LIVERPOOL (＿＿＿＿＿ I
CRICKETERS
1882-1947

compiled by

Don Ambrose

Published by the Association of Cricket Statisticians and Historians, West Bridgford, Nottingham
2002
Typeset by Limlow Books
Printed by Tranters, Derby
ISBN: 1 902171 66 7

ACKNOWLEDGMENTS

I wish to thank the following for assistance given to me during the research and production of this book: Philip Thorn, Peter Griffiths and Andrew Anderson (ACS), Doreen Ainscough and Ken Lea (Ormskirk), Peter Hall (Sefton), Chris Elston (Birkenhead Park), Tony Percival (Cheshire), Tom Law (Bootle), John Wylie and Ray Tyler (Liverpool), Jen Booth (The Rossallian Club), Mrs M.E.Griffiths (Sedbergh School), Mr T.W.Hildrey (Merchant Taylors' School, Crosby), Mr James Lawson (Old Salopian Club) and that walking encyclopaedia of Liverpool cricket Harold Wolfe.

INTRODUCTION

The first record of cricket being played in the Liverpool area asserts that it was on the Mersey Bowmen's Ground in Cazneau Street, near the City centre. This site is now occupied by the Liverpool Municipal Buildings and car park.

In 1807 a group of young men got together to form "The Original and Unrivalled Mosslake Fields Cricket Society", the original rules of which are still held by the Liverpool Cricket Club. They reveal that matches were held on the mornings of Monday, Wednesday and Friday. Members were expected to attend at six o'clock in the morning and if quarter of an hour late were fined six pence, the fines rising to 1s.6d. by seven o'clock and two shillings in the event of non-attendance. A cow-house served as a pavilion and dressing room and for refreshment they had readily available milk. It must be remembered that with long working hours, Saturday a full working day and no opportunity for organised sport on Sunday, early morning was the only chance to play and "Break of Day" or "Peep o' Dawn" clubs were common in urban areas until the late nineteenth century. There was at first little opportunity for matches against other clubs and usually sides were picked amongst members as they turned up.

Mosslake Fields, as the name suggests, could be very wet and poorly drained and wickets would be prepared where practicable, the driest area being between Crown Street and Smithdown Lane. The Fields adjoined the Botanical Gardens that had been opened by Roscoe in 1802, and were to the east of Abercrombie Square.

Liverpool Cricket Club was established in May 1811 and a copy of the Laws of Cricket for 1809, held by the Liverpool Record Office, records this fact. In the 18th October 1811 edition of *The Liverpool Mercury* a poem appeared under the title of "L.C.C." It ran to eighteen stanzas, one of which ran –

> "On Mersey's banks a town there lies,
> Where may be found immense supplies,
> Of youths both young and active:
> Who like their business passing well,
> And yet, if truth historians tell,
> Find pleasure more attractive."

The club continued to play on Mosslake Fields until 1819, when being on the edge of the Town, they were overtaken by the building of the new, fashionable, Georgian streets and squares. For the season of 1820 they moved a few hundred yards to Rector's Fields, which was situated in Crabtree Lane, later to be renamed Falkner Street. While at this ground the first match against Cheshire was played in 1822 and against Manchester in 1823. In September 1822 a match was played at Knowsley Park, the seat of Lord Derby. Membership of the club was limited to fifty members.

In 1829, yet again overtaken by the builders, the club had to move, this time over half a mile to the then peaceful and rural area of Edge Hill, in Wavertree Road. It was described as "a beautiful avenue lined with tall trees on each side, the foliage meeting overhead". A ditch separated the road from the enclosure, and although the centre of the field was smooth turf, beyond that area was bumpy and rough. All hits had to be run out, except those to the pavilion which counted three. Adjoining the ground was the "Half-way House", originally an old picturesque thatched cottage called the "Pump House", but subsequently converted into a public-house with tea-gardens and a skittle alley. It was here that the players changed and stored their equipment.

The last match played on this ground was on 6th September 1845, as the club had yet again been overtaken by a fast expanding Liverpool. A road, leading to Edge Hill Station, was cut though the ground, and in 1857 Arrow, Ash, Ryder and Speke Streets were built. In 1881 the remaining portion of the ground became the Fruit and Vegetable Depot for the London and North Western Railway.

The fourth ground was a quarter of a mile further out of town, just to the East of Edge Hill Station and its railway sidings. The ground was opened on 22nd May 1847 and in the September of that year it was the venue for a match between Fourteen of Liverpool v All England Eleven. Further matches against the All England Eleven took place in 1858 and 1859, and against the United All England Eleven in 1857.

Perhaps of greater social significance, however, was the first fixture against I Zingari in 1859. The social standing of the Liverpool Club had always been high, its membership being drawn from the professional and merchant families of the area. By 1860 fixtures against the major Public Schools were being made, and the club's famous Public School Tour started in 1866 and lasted until the First World War. Four Important or First-Class matches were played on this ground -

1859. Gentlemen of the North v Gentlemen of the South.
1863. North v South.
1866. Lancashire v Surrey.
1872. North v South (with W.G.Grace as captain).

The status of the club was considerably increased during their time at this ground and when the inevitable happened and they were again threatened by builders they were able to plan the purchase of a suitable alternative, this time far enough from the town centre to be safe. The encroachment of the railway sidings and gas works led to the grounds closure at the end of the 1877 season. A few years later the site of the ground was marked by the streets of Spofforth Road, Bannerman Street, Darling Street, Giffen Street and Murdoch Street, names not without significance to any cricket enthusiast. The Spofforth Public House still shows the connection with a portrait of the 'Demon Bowler' on its sign.

Now for a period of three years the club were without a ground while its new premises at Aigburth was prepared. Games were played on the beautiful ground at Croxteth Hall, the seat of their member Lord Sefton, for one year and at Childwall for two years. Practice wickets were made available at other Liverpool clubs at Childwall and Dingle and also at Birkenhead Park.

Liverpool in the 1880s

Liverpool in the 1880s was at the peak of its prosperity. A prosperity founded on the slave-trade and the opening up of trade links to the Americas, Africa and the West Indies. By the 1880s the slave-trade was a thing of the past, but world-wide trade links had grown to the Far East and Australasia. Massive imports of raw materials and exports of manufactured goods had led to the growth of the dock systems on the Liverpool side of the river both North and South of the city centre and also on the Cheshire side at Birkenhead and Wallasey. Ports further up the river also expanded at Port Sunlight, Bromborough, Ellesmere Port, Runcorn and Garston and the proposed new ship-canal to Manchester was at last under construction. Supporting this expansion was a large ship-building and repairing facility and factories for the process of raw materials into the finished product in vegetable oils, sugar, leather, timber, etc. Large quantities of cattle were imported from Ireland on the hoof and slaughtered at the dockside in Birkenhead. The Corn, Cotton and Stock Exchanges prospered as did the support industries of banking and insurance. Most of the largest shipping companies were represented in the city and many had made Liverpool their headquarters.

Distribution of goods from the docks had in the early years depended on a network of canals but there was by now a comprehensive rail network on both sides of the river, linked by the Mersey Railway tunnel for passenger trains, which opened 1st February 1886.

Although largely a working-class city, with large populations of Irish and Welsh incomers, there was a steady growth of the affluent middle-class. They were not content with the cramped and increasingly unhygienic city centre as a place to live and had since the arrival of the railways moved out to the more congenial suburbs. As the rail network grew on both sides of the river the railway companies and local landowners combined to offer new estates of Victorian villas adjoining new railway stations for the first commuters. In the 1850s and 1860s advertisements appeared in the local newspapers offering the sale of houses in the new suburbs with, as an incentive to buy, first-class one or two year contracts to a central Liverpool railway terminus.

The new estates growing up around the new railway stations led to a growth of local amenities, including sports and social clubs. The new cricket clubs in the suburbs led to a wider range of fixtures for the older, longer established clubs nearer to the city centre and based on these fixtures the Liverpool Competition was formed. This was never a league, the tables of merit were the work of the local press not the clubs, it was no more than a convenient grouping for ease of fixtures, with the participating clubs having room for local and traditional fixtures outside the magic circle. The drift towards standardised fixture lists with each team playing the same number of matches and a full league structure was only completed after the Second World War.

The Aigburth Ground

Liverpool Cricket Club's move to Aigburth was well timed to take advantage of this situation. The ground, surrounded by green fields and farms enjoyed uninterrupted views across the river to the Wirral and the Welsh mountains beyond. The Cheshire Lines Committee main line railway from Manchester to Liverpool Central station formed one boundary to the property, suitably hidden in a deep cutting. Express trains took only 40 minutes for the journey from Liverpool to Manchester and the stopping train 15 minutes from Liverpool to Cressington and Grassendale station which was only five minutes walk to the back gate of the cricket club. Trains from that station to Manchester took 45 minutes. The line had opened in 1864 but was only extended into Central station Liverpool in 1874 and it was only then that Fulwood, Grassendale and Cressington Parks were fully developed as housing estates. The city's tramway system only reached Aigburth Vale just over a mile from the cricket ground and was extended to the ground in August 1902 when Liverpool Corporation took over the still uncompleted line from Garston to Aigburth.

The pavilion dominates the ground and reflects the pride and prosperity of the City of Liverpool and the Liverpool Cricket Club in 1881. It must be remembered that the present pavilion at Lord's was only opened in 1891, and that at Old Trafford, Manchester in 1894. The Liverpool pavilion ranked amongst the very best in England.

The Lancashire County Cricket Club was formed at a meeting at the Queens Hotel, Manchester, on 12th January 1864. At that meeting there were thirteen Lancashire cricket clubs represented; ten members from the Manchester club attended, four from the Western Club, Eccles, two from Longsight, two from Ashton-under-Lyne and four from the Manchester Broughton Club. Liverpool had four representatives, Huyton and Northern one each. Blackburn with two representatives and Accrington, Oldham, Whalley and Wigan with one each completed the numbers. In spite of the dominance of the Manchester contingent the meeting was chaired by W.Horner of the Liverpool club and it was agreed that subscriptions should be invited from clubs throughout the county. It was also agreed that matches should be played in different parts of the county, but Sam Swire, the secretary of the Manchester Club disagreed, and feeling the Old Trafford should be the ground for all matches

5

and Manchester should be the headquarters, refused to serve on the committee. He was later to join the committee as secretary and his views were adopted. Liverpool got a steady supply of matches from the Gentlemen of Lancashire – Lancashire without professionals – but the only first-class Lancashire match was that against Surrey in 1866. Whalley got the first 'Roses Match' in 1867 and Castleton, Rochdale the match against Kent in 1876, but all other home matches were played at Old Trafford.

It was hoped in Liverpool that with their fine new ground more fixtures would be allocated to Aigburth. On 13th and 14th June 1882 Lancashire played Cambridge University in the first first-class match to be played on the ground. Lancashire lost by seven wickets, due it was said to the wicket not yet being up to standard. Allan Steel, the Liverpool all-rounder played for his University and took eleven wickets for 91 runs. It was Lancashire's only defeat of the season.

The following year Liverpool were allocated the match against Nottinghamshire and decided to widen their fixture list by forming a Liverpool and District team with which to play the Australian tourists. This was the first of fourteen matches played by the Liverpool & District side between 1882 and 1894, which were advertised as being first-class and were counted in the players first-class averages by all the sporting press. A ruling on the status of future fixtures was sought from the MCC in 1895 and they were ruled to be not first-class. A ruling on matches already played was never sought or given and the scores have always been counted into the first-class averages.

Throughout the time that the team operated they were strongly supported by the Steel brothers, four of whom appeared for the team. Allan Steel played in all fourteen of the first-class matches, but in none of the others. The amateurs nearly all had other first-class experience or at least played with a second-class county. The professionals were drawn from the many strong clubs in the area and from the pool of professional talent at the Liverpool club itself. Of the fourteen matches played three were won, three drawn and eight lost. Not a bad record considering the strength of the opposition.

Regular fixtures were played by the Liverpool and District team until 1920 without first-class status, although some were advertised as having this status, and the difference in standard in one or two cases is marginal. Two additional Liverpool and District XI matches were played in 1932 and 1947.

Half a dozen matches were played by Gentlemen of Liverpool XIs between 1884 and 1911 against the weaker touring sides.

The matches played were well supported, with attendances in excess of ten thousand being reported. Stands were built on both sides of the ground and a Ladies pavilion was also constructed. In addition to cricket, lawn tennis and quoits were also played and the club operated as a gentlemen's dining club, with tables for dinner having to be reserved by members well in advance. A close connection was formed with the Liverpool Rugby Football Club which lasted until that club merged with St.Helens and moved to a ground in that area.

Throughout the 1880s and 1890s the Liverpool cricket club maintained a group of professional players, primarily as ground bowlers and for practice, but one or two were used to supplement their sides in the stronger fixtures. The public school connection remained throughout the 20s and 30s but slowly the club was forced to widen its membership. It is usually allocated one or two fixtures per year from the Lancashire County Cricket Club with which they maintain close and friendly links. The tennis, crown green bowls, quoits and squash sections continue and the pavilion is the headquarters of the Old Collegiate Rugby Union Club.

FIRST-CLASS MATCHES PLAYED BY LIVERPOOL & DISTRICT

31st July, 1st & 2nd August 1882. Australians 240 (Giffen 81, Horan 70, Crossland 7-72) and 6-1 drew with Liverpool & District 112 (A.G.Steel 50, Boyle 5-51, Palmer 5-60) and 137 (C.L.Jones 36, Boyle 6-56, Palmer 4-73).

23rd & 24th June 1884. Liverpool & District 213 (A.G.Steel 72, Boyle 5-33) and 54 (A.G.Steel 29, Boyle 5-24, Palmer 5-29) lost to Australians 140 (Giffen 36, Crossland 5-50) and 128-9 (Murdoch 38*, Crossland 6-20) by one wicket.

16th & 17th July 1886. Australians 152 (McIlwraith 34*, A.G.Steel 4-46) and 141-8 (Scott 80, E.C.Hornby 2-23) drew with Liverpool & District 204 (A.G.Steel 55, Bruce 3-27).

23rd, 24th & 25th June 1887. Liverpool & District 137 (A.G.Steel 44, Preston 3-21) and 259 (A.G.Steel 68, Richardson 55, Peel 4-58) beat Yorkshire 248 (Wade 47, A.G.Steel 4-61) and 110 (Bates 32, Richardson 6-58) by 38 runs.

2nd, 3rd & 4th July 1888. Australians 119 (Jarvis 27, E.Smith 4-39) and 150 (Bonnor 46, Richardson 7-46) beat Liverpool & District 70 (E.C.Hornby 28, Worrall 5-20, Turner 5-40) and 69 (H.B.Steel 31, Turner 6-36) by 130 runs.

30th & 31st May & 1st June 1889. Liverpool & District 145 (A.G.Steel 33, Peel 7-69) and 45 (E.Smith 16, Peel 5-8, Wade 5-34) lost to Yorkshire 231 (Lee 84, Ulyett 65, F.J.Jones 4-71) by an innings and 41 runs.

15th, 16th & 17th July 1889. M.Sherwin's Nottinghamshire XI 186 (Redgate 37, W.Price 6-51) and 15-1 beat Liverpool & District 80 (H.M.Grayson 42, Attewell 5-32, Flowers 5-26) and 119 (A.G.Steel 59, Flowers 6-53, Attewell 4-48) by nine wickets.

22nd, 23rd & 24th May 1890. Yorkshire 107 (Hunter 28*, Bretherton 5-30) and 181 (Ulyett 38, Bretherton 3-44, A.G.Steel 3-53) beat Liverpool & District 78 (Crosfield 27, Peel 7-35) and 137 (Champion 24, Peel 3-35, Wainwright 3-35, Wade 3-43) by 73 runs.

18th, 19th & 20th June 1891. Liverpool & District 269 (A.G.Steel 100, Bretherton 50, Ulyett 3-31) and 217 (H.B.Steel 48, Peel 4-55) beat Yorkshire 271 (Ulyett 54, Bretherton 4-88) and 161 (Hall 54, E.Smith 7-59) by 54 runs.

11th, 12th & 13th July 1892. Liverpool & District 230 (Hubback 67, Hall 4-51) and 197-4 (MacLaren 84, Ainscough 61*, Mounsey 2-21, Hirst 2-50) beat Yorkshire 69 (Hawke 18, Oakley 5-29, Bretherton 4-29) and 354 (Wardall 112, Hall 101, Oakley 5-113) by six wickets.

15th, 16th & 17th May 1893. Yorkshire 309 (Franks 92, J.T.Brown 68, E.Smith 4-83) drew with Liverpool & District 205 (MacLaren 47, Walton 3-93) and 172 (MacLaren 49, Wainwright 4-62).

10th, 11th & 12th August 1893. Australians 195 (Trott 56, Oakley 5-50) beat Liverpool & District 85 (H.B.Steel 21, McLeod 7-24, Coningham 3-59) and 76 (Stubbs 17, Coningham 6-41, McLeod 3-32) by an innings and 34 runs.

21st, 22nd & 23rd June 1894. Liverpool & District 153 (Ainscough 50, Foster 5-45) and 154 (A.G.Steel 70, Foster 6-48) lost to Yorkshire 306 (J.T.Brown 141, A.G.Steel 4-70) and 4-0 by ten wickets.

12th, 13th & 14th July 1894. Liverpool & District 87 (MacLaren 34, Gray 7-56) and 185 (Stubbs 43, Robinson 5-58, Gray 4-51) lost to Cambridge University 191 (Brunton 54, A.Smith 4-57) and 84-1 (Ranjitsinhji 41*) by nine wickets.

NON FIRST-CLASS MATCHES PLAYED BY
GENTLEMEN OF LIVERPOOL (& DISTRICT)

7th & 8th July 1884. Gentlemen of Philadelphia 185 (Scott 93, E.E.Steel 4-50) and 102 (R.S.Newhall 52, Wood 4-35) beat Gentlemen of Liverpool 169 (H.B.Steel 77, C.A.Newhall 5-54) and 114 (Parr 46, Lowry 6-16) by 4 runs.

22nd & 23rd August 1887. Gentlemen of Liverpool & District 233 (Holden 64, H.B.Steel 54, W.W.Jones 3-44) and 76-4 (C.L.Jones 29*, Ferrie 2-35) beat Gentlemen of Canada 78 (Henry 48, Evans 5-36) and 229 (Henry 69, Evans 6-58) by six wickets.

23rd & 24th July 1888. Parsees 51 (Eranee 19, Ashworth 5-23, Eccles 5-25) and 134 (P.D.Kanga 23, Ashworth 4-37, Eccles 4-36) lost to Gentlemen of Liverpool 130 (Roper 41, M.D.Kanga 3-13, Pandole 3-55) and 56-5 (Bird 15, P.D.Kanga 2-5, M.D.Kanga 2-28) by five wickets.

11th & 12th July 1889. Gentlemen of Philadelphia 445 (Scott 125, R.D.Brown 102, Morgan 63, E.C.Hornby 5-86) beat Gentlemen of Liverpool 123 (Nicholson 30*, Patterson 8-30) and 170 (E.C.Hornby 64, Scott 5-55) by an innings and 152 runs.

30th June & 1st July 1910. Toronto Zingari 164 (Southam 57, Rimmer 4-55) and 99 (Southam 40, Hannay 7-31) lost to Gentlemen of Liverpool & District 167 (Morrice 50, Gibson, Greening and Rathburn 3 wickets each) and 97-5 (Hannay 28, Gibson 3 wickets) by 5 wickets.

18th & 19th August 1911. Gentlemen of Liverpool 117 (Cunningham 37, O'Neill 6 wickets) and 96 (Barnes 40, Clark 4 wickets) lost to Germantown 382 (Jordan 106, Priestman 72, Clark 53, O'Neill 50, Rimmer 5-89) by an innings and 169 runs.

NON FIRST-CLASS MATCHES PLAYED
BY LIVERPOOL & DISTRICT

19th, 20th & 21st July 1894. Liverpool & District 110 (Lorrimer 48, Rowe 5-52) and 207 (Kemble 39, Rowe 4-88) lost to South Africans (Johnson 112, Davey 50*, A.Smith 4-56) and 31-3 (Routledge 22*) by seven wickets.

16th, 17th & 18th May 1895. Liverpool & District 235 (Ainscough 61, Stubbs 50, Hirst 4-81) and 91-3 (Stubbs 45*) beat Yorkshire 99 (Hirst 22, Bretherton 8-42) and 226 (Frank 73*, Ringrose 5-64) by seven wickets.

11th, 12th & 13th July 1895. Cambridge University 403 (Mitchell 155, Druce 58, Bretherton 5-121, Oakley 5-132) beat Liverpool & District 47 (Hubback 13, Gray 6-26) and 184 (Kemble 59, C.E.M.Wilson 4-48) by an innings and 172 runs.

9th & 10th July 1896. Liverpool & District 127 (Hutton 65*, Jessop 3-37) and 226 (Barnes 85, Holden 63, Jessop 5-91) beat Cambridge University 71 (Bray 18, Ringrose 8-47) and 137 (Garnett 29*, Ringrose 8-68) by 145 runs.

8th, 9th & 10th July 1897. Liverpool & District 399 (Holden 172, F.Sugg 55, Ainscough 51, C.E.M.Wilson 5-37) and 172 (Barnes 53, C.E.M.Wilson 8-61) drew with Cambridge University 290 (Druce 163, Barnes 3-30, Oakley 3-67) and 203-9 (Mitchell 43, King 3-26, Barnes 3-46).

4th, 5th & 6th July 1898. Cambridge University 400 (Winter 142, Coode 117, Stoddart 4-115) and 60-0 (Mitchell 51*) beat Liverpool & District 218 (Leach 41, Hawkins, 6-38) and 239 (Barnes 54, C.E.M.Wilson 5-64) by ten wickets.

6th, 7th & 8th July 1899. Liverpool & District 212 (H.B.Steel 58, Hawkins 4-70) and 225 (Stoddart 56*, Hawkins 4-40) beat Cambridge University 107 (Taylor 24, Stoddart 5-43) and 130 (Jessop 43, Stoddart 6-78) by 200 runs.

9th & 10th July 1900. Liverpool & District 208 (Burrough 62, Stoddart 56*, Dowson 8-78) and 263 (H.G.Garnett 97, Dowson 5-94) lost to Cambridge University 431 (Day 153, Druce 124, Taylor 68, Burrough 4-73, Ringrose 4-90) and 43-2 by eight wickets.

2nd, 3rd & 4th August 1900. West Indians 265 (Sproston 118, Cox 76, Gregory 5-111, Burrough 4-60) and 124-5 declared (Goodman 42*, Burrough 4-42) drew with Liverpool & District 218 (Holden 86, Cox 54, Burton 5-98) and 100-0 (Pilkington 68*).

24th & 25th June 1901. Liverpool & District 141 (Ainscough 38, Llewellyn 6-51) and 189 (Ainscough 53, Llewellyn 6-79) lost to South Africans 127 (Llewellyn 51, Kitchener 4-37, E.E.Steel 4-37) and 204-5 (Tancred 56, Hathorn 55, E.E.Steel 2-49) by five wickets.

8th, 9th & 10th July 1901. Liverpool & District 315 (H.B.Steel 91, E.E.Steel 77, Dowson 3-80, E.R.Wilson 3-87) and 304 (H.B.Steel 91*, H.G.Garnett 68, Dowson 9-120) lost to Cambridge University 377 (Robertson 103, J.Stanning 64, Burnup 59, Warren 4-114) and 244-5 (Robertson 90, Burnup 68, E.E.Steel 3-36) by five wickets.

1st, 2nd & 3rd August 1901. Liverpool & District 321 (H.G.Garnett 81, E.C.Hornby 70, Leather 67, H.Jessop 4-57) and 421 (Ainscough 195, H.G.Garnett 90, Spry 6-133) beat G.L.Jessop's Gloucestershire XI 312 (Rice 144, G.L.Jessop 79, Kitchener 5-110) and 310 (G.L.Jessop 140, Kitchener 4-82, Bowring 4-87) by 120 runs.

7th, 8th & 9th July 1902. Liverpool & District 334 (Ainscough 88, Cole 88, Burroughs 55, Penn 3-76, E.R.Wilson 3-76) and 243 (Cole 61, Bardswell 51*, E.R.Wilson 4-87) drew with Cambridge University 218 (Burnup 104, Kitchener 6-86) and 256-6 (Ebden 65, Penn 58*, Burnup 50, Rimmer 3-64).

30th & 31st July, 1st August 1902. Liverpool & District 225 (Barnes 86, Roberts 4-29) and 133 (Leather 23, Huggins 6-78) lost to G.L.Jessop's Gloucestershire XI 208 (Langdon 69, Rimmer 4-78) and 151-5 (Wrathall 45, Kitchener 2-45) by five wickets.

18th & 19th May 1903. S.M.J.Woods' Somerset XI 279 (Braund 117, Lewis 69, E.E.Steel 3-40; Rimmer 3-74) beat Liverpool & District 64 (E.E.Steel 28, Cranfield 6-26) and 98 (Taylor 17, Woods 3-20) by an innings and 117 runs.

6th, 7th & 8th July 1903. Liverpool & District 222 (Cole 62, McDonell 5-53) and 390 (Cole 116, E.E.Steel 62, Roberts 3-57, McDonell 3-83) beat Cambridge University 166 (Marriott 53, E.E.Steel 6-48) and 252 (Marriott 122, E.E.Steel 7-95) by 194 runs.

4th, 5th & 6th July 1904. Liverpool & District 282 (Warlow 54, Hancock 50, Napier 4-64) and 170 (A.F.Spooner 42, Hollender 4-51) lost to Cambridge University 147 (Mann 27, E.E.Steel 6-65) and 306-4 (Harris 92*, Weaver 59, Keigwin 58, Barnes 2-48) by six wickets.

21st & 22nd July 1904. South Africans 324 (Mitchell 87*, Hathorn 68, Snooke 50, Brown 4-81) beat Liverpool & District 111 (A.F.Spooner 50, Schwarz 5-40) and 118 (Ainscough 34, Kotze 6-53) by an innings and 95 runs.

10th, 11th & 12th July 1905. Cambridge University 208 (Keigwin 62, Young 50, Kitchener 3-45) and 249 (Young 125, Page 50, Thompson 6-55) lost to Liverpool & District 181 (Hancock 45, Morcom 4-63) and 278-3 (Morrice 91*, C.E.Wilson 78*, Morcom 2-75) by seven wickets.

9th, 10th & 11th July 1906. Cambridge University 421 (Young 114, Mugliston 112, Court 4-74, Rimmer 4-119) and 139 (Payne 40, Mason 6-24) beat Liverpool & District 285 (Graham 86, Barnes 84, Keigwin 4-58) and 203 (McCormick 61, Morcom 4-38) by 72 runs.

8th, 9th & 10th July 1907. Cambridge University 200 (Buchanan 66, Stoddart 5-40) and 126 (Magnay 40, Stoddart 4-39, Brown 4-45) drew with Liverpool & District 105 (Brown 20, Goodwin 6-48) and 204-9 (Barnes 80, C.F.Lyttelton 5-60).

12th, 13th & 14th July 1920. Liverpool & District 153 (J.R.Barnes 41, Browne 4-25, Marriott 4-66) and 166 (J.R.Barnes 48, Marriott 5-71, Browne 4-52) beat Cambridge University 92 (Brocklebank 30, Blackburne 6-50, Cunningham 4-23) and 104 (Brooke-Taylor 51, Cunningham 5-41, Blackburne 4-41) by 123 runs.

11th & 12th July 1932. South Americans 337-2 declared (D.Ayling 127, A.L.S.Jackson 123, A.Nutter 1-41) and 72-3 (Knox 47, Barrell 1-19) drew with Liverpool & District 375 (W.E.Bates 111, H.S.Brown 67, H.W.Hodgson 56, Knox 4-46).

4th, 5th & 6th June 1947. Lancashire 313 (G.A.Edrich 101, Washbrook 63, Shepherd 5-73) drew with Liverpool & District 91 (Wolstenholme 24, Phillipson 3-27) and 158-7 (Lister 54, Price 4-13).

CRICKETERS WHO PLAYED FOR LIVERPOOL & DISTRICT IN FIRST-CLASS MATCHES

AINSCOUGH, Thomas (1891-94) b Lancaster House, Parbold, Lancashire 23.2.1865. d Lancaster House, Parbold, Lancashire 20.11.1927. ed Ampleforth. Brother of Hugh (Liverpool & District 1895 - not first-class) and John (Liverpool & District 1895 - not first-class). Lancashire (1894-1906), Liverpool & District (1894-1904 - not first-class). lhb. Club: Ormskirk.

ASPINALL, Frederick (1892) b West Kirby, Cheshire 2.9.1859. Cheshire (1886-92). Club: Birkenhead Park.

BARLOW, Richard Gorton (1882-84) b Barrow Bridge, Bolton, Lancashire 29.5.1851. d Blackpool, Lancashire 31.7.1919. Lancashire (1871-91), England (17 Tests). rhb. lm. Tours: to Australia 1881/82, 1882/83, 1886/87. First-class umpire.

BRETHERTON, James (1890-94) b Whiston, Lancashire 5.1.1862. d Raby, Wirral, Cheshire 9.6.1926. ed Mount St.Mary's, Chesterfield. Brother of T.R. (Cheshire 1890-94). Cheshire (1889-91), Liverpool & District (1895-98 - not first-class). rhb. rm. Clubs: Rock Ferry, Chester Boughton Hall.

BRIGGS, John (1882-84) b Sutton-in-Ashfield, Nottinghamshire 3.10.1862. d Heald Green, Cheadle, Cheshire 11.1.1902. Son of James (professional at Widnes 1877-92), brother of Joseph B. (Nottinghamshire 1888). Lancashire (1879-1900), England (33 Tests). rhb. sla. Tours: to Australia 1884/85, 1886/87, 1887/88, 1891/92, 1894/95, 1897/98, to South Africa 1888/89. Club: Northern Waterloo.

BRUTTON, Rev. Ernest Bartholomew (1892) b Tynemouth, Newcastle-upon-Tyne, Northumberland 29.7.1864. d Aylesbeare, Devon 19.4.1922. ed Durham. Brother of Septimus (Hampshire 1904), uncle of C.P. (Hampshire 1921-30). C.I.Thornton's XI (1885), Northumberland (1881-91), Devon (1901-14). rhb. rf. Rugby: Cambridge University (blue) and England, athletics: Cambridge University (blue). Club: Liverpool.

CHAMBERS, Charles Graham (1894) b West Isley, Wantage, Berkshire 12.7.1870. d Reading, Berkshire 30.1.1921. ed Marlborough, Oxford University. Cheshire (1894), Dorset (1896). rhb. Club: Chester Boughton Hall.

CHAMPION, Albert (1889-90) b Hollins End, Handsworth, Yorkshire 27.12.1851. d Wortley, Sheffield, Yorkshire 30.6.1909. Yorkshire (1876-90), Lancashire (1886). lhb. rm. Club: Sefton.

CHAPMAN, Mat (1893) b Arnesby, Leicestershire 13.4.1865. d Narborough, Leicestershire 28.11.1909. Leicestershire (1894-95). rhb. wk/rm. Club: Birkenhead Park.

COX, George Robert (1884) b Twickenham, Middlesex 9.11.1859. d Hoylake, Cheshire 24.2.1936. ed Uppingham. Brother of A.R. (Cambridge University 1887). rhb. Club: Liverpool.

CROSFIELD, Sydney Morland (1890) b Warrington, Lancashire 12.11.1861. d Las Palmas, Canary Islands 30.1.1908. ed Wimbledon. Lancashire (1883-99), Cheshire (1880-82), Liverpool & District (1895 - not first-class) rhb. rf/rs. Clubs: Lymm, Warrington, Sefton.

CROSSLAND, John (1882-84) b Sutton-in-Ashfield, Nottinghamshire 2.4.1852. d Blackburn, Lancashire 26.9.1903. Lancashire (1878-85), C.I.Thornton's XI (1887). rf. Club: Manchester.

DISNEY, James Joseph (1894) b Butterley, Derbyshire 20.11.1859. d Ripley, Derbyshire 24.6.1934. Derbyshire (1881-87), Cheshire (1893-95). rhb. wk. Club: Stockport.

DOBELL, Percy (1886-88) b Huyton, Liverpool 29.4.1864. d Freshfield, Formby, Lancashire 5.1.1903. ed Birkenhead, Cambridge University. Lancashire (1886-87). Club: Huyton.

DURANDU, Arthur (1887) b Great Crosby, Liverpool, Lancashire 25.12.1860. d Great Crosby, Liverpool, Lancashire 4.2.1903. Lancashire (1887). Club: Northern Waterloo.

ECCLES, Henry (1889) b Huyton Park, Liverpool, Lancashire 4.3.1863. d Roby, Liverpool, Lancashire 10.2.1931. ed Uppingham. Brother of A.P. (Gentlemen of Liverpool 1888). Lancashire (1885-86). rhb. rf. Club: Huyton.

EVANS, Thomas (1886-89) b Stoneyford, Codnor, Derbyshire 3.6.1852. d Heaton Moor, Lancashire 2.12.1916. Brother of Harry (Derbyshire 1878-82). Derbyshire (1883), Gentlemen of Liverpool (1887). rhb. rsm. Club: Sefton.

FIELDWICK, Edward (1894) b Huyton, Liverpool, Lancashire 25.3.1868. d Huyton, Liverpool, Lancashire 22.12.1910. Club: Huyton.

GRAYSON, Henry Mulleneux (1884-90) b Liverpool, Lancashire 26.6.1865. d Marylebone, London 27.10.1951. ed Winchester. Brother of J.H.F. (Liverpool & District 1891-93, Cheshire 1892-93, Liverpool & District 1895 - not first-class). Cheshire (1884-92). rhb. wk. Became a baronet 1922. Club: Birkenhead Park.

GRAYSON, John Hubert FitzHenry (1891-93) b West Derby, Liverpool, Lancashire 17.6.1871. d Eastbourne, Sussex 31.5.1936. ed Radley. Brother of Sir H.M. (Liverpool & District 1884-92, Cheshire 1884-92). Cheshire (1892-93), Liverpool & District (1895 - not first-class) rhb. rm. Club: Birkenhead Park.

HANDFORD, Alick (1894) b Wilford, Nottinghamshire 3.5.1869. d Tavistock, Devon 15.10.1935. Brother of Saunders (Players of USA 1892). Players of USA (1892), Nottinghamshire (1894-98), MCC (1901), Southland (1914/15), Liverpool & District (1894 - not first-class). rhb. rm. Club: Sefton.

HENSON Richard (1894) b Ruddington, Nottinghamshire 10.10.1864. d Ruddington, Nottinghamshire 29.11.1930. Liverpool & District (1898 - not first-class). lsm. Club: Northern Waterloo.

HOLDEN, Cecil (1886-91) b West Derby, Liverpool, Lancashire 1.6.1865. d Claughton, Birkenhead, Cheshire 22.8.1928. Lancashire (1890), Cheshire (1884-95), Gentlemen of Liverpool (1887), Liverpool & District (1895-1901 - not first-class). rhb. rm. Club: Birkenhead Park.

HORNBY, Edgar Christian (1886-94) b Wavertree, Liverpool, Lancashire 14.9.1863. d Claygate, Surrey 2.4.1922. Brother of G.F. (Oxford University 1882, Gentlemen of Liverpool 1884) and Joseph (Gentlemen of Liverpool 1889), father of A.H. (Europeans 1934/35). ed Winchester. Lancashire (1885-87), Gentlemen of Liverpool (1884-89), Liverpool & District (1901 - not first-class). lhb. sla. Club: Liverpool.

HUBBACK, Theodore Rathbone (1892-93) b Liverpool, Lancashire 17.12.1872. d Malaya 1942. Lancashire (1892), Liverpool & District (1895 - not first-class). wk. Club: Dingle.

JONES, Charles Langton (1882-90) b Sefton, Liverpool, Lancashire 27.11.1853. d Toxteth Park, Liverpool, Lancashire 2.4.1904. Brother of F.J. (Liverpool & District 1889). Lancashire (1876-88), Gentlemen of Liverpool (1887). rhb. rm. Club: Sefton.

JONES, Frederic John (1889) b West Derby, Liverpool, Lancashire 2.11.1850. d Liverpool, Lancashire 9.6.1921. Brother of C.L. (Lancashire 1876-88, Liverpool & District 1882-90; Gentlemen of Liverpool 1887). rf. Club: Sefton.

KEMBLE, Arthur Twiss (1887-94) b Sebergham, Carlisle, Cumberland 3.2.1862. d Crawley Down, Sussex 13.3.1925. Lancashire (1885-94), West of England (1896); Cumberland (1889), Gentlemen of Liverpool (1887-89), Liverpool & District (1894-1903 - not first-class). Rugby: Lancashire and England. rhb. wk. Secretary of the Liverpool CC for many years. Club: Liverpool.

LEACH, Harold (1884-91) b Lower Fold, Rochdale, Lancashire 13.3.1862. d Widcombe, Bath, Somerset 15.2.1928. ed Marlborough. Brother of John (Lancashire 1866-77), Robert (Lancashire 1866-77), R.C. (Lancashire 1885), W.E. (Lancashire 1885, Canterbury 1876/77). Lancashire (1881), Gentlemen of Liverpool (1889), Liverpool & District (1898 - not first-class). rhb. sra. Clubs: Liverpool, Dingle.

MacLAREN, Archibald Campbell (1892-94) b Whalley Range, Manchester, Lancashire 1.12.1871. d Warfield Park, Bracknell, Berkshire 17.11.1944. ed Harrow. Brother of Dr.J.A. (Lancashire 1891-94) and G. (Lancashire 1902). His mother married A.B.Rowley (Lancashire 1865-71, Cheshire 1863-69) in 1901. Lancashire (1890-1914), England (35 Tests). Tours: to Australia 1894/95, 1897/98, 1901/02, to North America 1899, to South America 1911/12, to New Zealand and Australia 1922/23. rhb. rf. Club: Liverpool.

MORGAN, William Arthur (1889) b Everton, Liverpool, Lancashire 6.12.1864. d Cosham, Hampshire 3.4.1934. Clubs: Sefton, Stanley.

MOSS, Rev. Reginald Heber (1893) b Huyton, Liverpool, Lancashire 24.2.1868. d Bridport, Dorset 19.3.1956. ed Radley, Oxford University. Oxford University (1887-89), Worcestershire (1925), Bedfordshire (1901-09), Herefordshire (1907). Athletics: Oxford University (blue). rhb. rfm. Club: Huyton.

OAKLEY, William (1892-94) b Shrewsbury, Shropshire 6.5.1868. Lancashire (1893-94), Shropshire (1891-05), Liverpool & District (1895-97 - not first-class). lm. Club: Sefton.

PATTERSON, William Seeds (1882) b Mossley Hill, Liverpool, Lancashire 19.3.1854. d Hook Heath, Woking, Surrey 20.10.1939. ed Uppingham. Cambridge University (1874-77), Lancashire (1874-82), English Residents in America (1880-81). rhb. rm. Club: Liverpool.

PILLING, Richard (1882) b Old Warden, Bedfordshire 11.8.1855. d Old Trafford, Manchester, Lancashire 28.3.1891. Brother of William (Lancashire 1891). Lancashire (1877-89), England (8 Tests). Tours: to Australia 1881/82, 1887/88. rhb. wk. Club: Church.

PORTER, Edward Horatio (1882) b Liverpool, Lancashire 13.10.1846. d Hooton, Cheshire 31.10.1918. Lancashire (1874-82), Lancashire & Yorkshire (1883). rhb. rm. Club: Birkenhead Park.

PRICE, Alfred (1884) b Ruddington, Nottinghamshire 5.1.1862. d Mumps, Oldham, Lancashire 21.3.1942. Son of Walter (Nottinghamshire 1869-70), brother of Frederick (North 1887) and William (Liverpool & District 1889; Liverpool & District 1896 - not first-class). North (1884), Lancashire (1885), Nottinghamshire (1887). rhb. Club: Liverpool.

PRICE, William (1889) b Ruddington, Nottinghamshire 4.12.1859. Son of Walter (Nottinghamshire 1869-70), brother of Alfred (North 1884, Lancashire 1885, Nottinghamshire 1887, Liverpool & District 1884) and Frederick (North 1887). Liverpool & District (1896 - not first-class). Clubs: Liverpool, Bootle.

RATCLIFFE, Edgar (1886-89) b Liverpool, Lancashire 19.1.1863. d Aston, Birmingham, Warwickshire 29.7.1915. Brother of Harold (Gentlemen of Liverpool 1887). Lancashire (1884). Club: Sefton.

RAVENSCROFT, James (1888-94) b Liverpool, Lancashire 9.12.1854. d Liverpool, Lancashire 3.1.1931. ed Rugby. Father of Leslie (Cheshire 1910). Cheshire (1883-95), Gentlemen of Liverpool (1887). rhb. Club: Rock Ferry.

RICHARDSON, Henry (1887-89) b Bulwell, Nottinghamshire 4.10.1857. d Bulwell, Nottinghamshire 20.3.1940. Nottinghamshire (1887-90). rhb. rm. Club: Liverpool.

ROPER, Edward (1891-93) b Richmond, Yorkshire 8.4.1851. d Toxteth, Liverpool, Lancashire 24.4.1921. ed Clifton. Lancashire (1876-86), Yorkshire (1878-80), Gentlemen of Liverpool (1884-88). Secretary of Sefton and Liverpool clubs. rhb. Clubs: Sefton, Liverpool.

ROYLE, Rev. Vernon Peter Fanshawe Archer (1882) b Brooklands, Cheshire 29.1.1854. d Stanmore Park, Middlesex 21.5.1929. ed Rossall. Oxford University (1875-76), Lancashire (1873-91), England (1878/9, 1 Test), Cheshire (1873-76). Tour: to Australia 1878/79. rhb. rsr-a. Clubs: Western, Free Foresters.

SHORE, Charles (1886-87) b Sutton-in-Ashfield, Nottinghamshire 21.11.1858. d Sutton-in-Ashfield, Nottinghamshire 5.6.1912. Nottinghamshire (1881-85), Lancashire (1886), Herefordshire (1886), Norfolk (1889-1901). lhb. sla. Club: Sefton.

SHOUBRIDGE, Thomas Edward (1890) b Horsham, Sussex 8.9.1868. d Prescot, Lancashire 22.10.1937. Sussex (1890). rfr-a. Club: Liverpool.

SMITH, Albert (1894) Cheshire (1894-95), Lancashire 2nd XI (1894). sla. Club: Oxton.

SMITH, Edwin (1886-94) b Peatling Magna, Leicestershire 11.6.1860. d Ashby Magna, Leicestershire 30.5.1939. Leicestershire (1884-86), Cheshire (1888-95), Lancashire 2nd XI (1892). rhb. rfm. Club: Birkenhead Park.

STEEL, Allan Gibson (1882-94) b West Derby, Liverpool, Lancashire 24.9.1858. d Hyde Park, London 15.6.1914. ed Marlborough. Brother of D.Q. (Cambridge University 1876-79, Lancashire 1876-87, Liverpool & District 1882-86), E.E. (Lancashire 1884-1903, Liverpool & District 1887-93, Europeans 1892/93, Gentlemen of Liverpool 1884, Liverpool & District 1901-07 - not first-class), H.B. (Lancashire 1883-96, Liverpool & District 1884-94, Gentlemen of Liverpool 1884-89, Liverpool & District 1894-1904 - not first-class), father of A.L. (Middlesex 1912). Lancashire (1877-93), Cambridge University (1878-81), England (1880-88, 13 Tests). Tour: to Australia 1882/83. rhb. rsm. He was President of MCC 1902. Clubs: Liverpool, I Zingari.

STEEL, Douglas Quentin (1882-86) b West Derby, Liverpool, Lancashire 19.6.1856. d Upton, Cheshire 2.12.1933. ed Uppingham. Brother of A.G. (Lancashire 1877-93, Cambridge University 1878-81, Liverpool & District 1882-94, England 1880-88), E.E. (Lancashire 1884-1903, Liverpool & District 1887-93, Europeans 1892/93, Gentlemen of Liverpool 1884, Liverpool & District 1901-07 - not first-class), H.B. (Lancashire 1883-96, Liverpool & District

1884-94, Gentlemen of Liverpool 1884-89, Liverpool & District 1894-1904 - not first-class), uncle of A.I. (Middlesex 1912). Cambridge University (1876-79), Lancashire (1876-87). rhb. rsr-a. wk. Club: Liverpool.

STEEL, Ernest Eden (1887-93) b West Derby, Liverpool, Lancashire 25.6.1864. d Southport, Lancashire 14.7.1941. ed Marlborough. Brother of A.G. (Lancashire 1877-93, Cambridge University 1878-81, Liverpool & District 1882-94, England 1880-88), D.Q. (Cambridge University 1876-79, Lancashire 1876-87, Liverpool & District 1882-86), H.B. (Lancashire 1883-96, Liverpool & District 1884-94, Gentlemen of Liverpool 1884-89, Liverpool & District 1894-1904 - not first-class), uncle of A.I. (Middlesex 1912). Lancashire (1884-1903), Europeans (1892/93): Gentlemen of Liverpool (1884), Liverpool & District (1901-07 - not first-class). rhb. sra. Club: Liverpool.

STEEL, Harold Banner (1884-94) b South Hill, Liverpool, Lancashire 9.4.1862. d Burnham, Somerset 29.6.1911. ed Repton, Uppingham and Cambridge University. Brother of A.G. (Lancashire 1877-93, Cambridge University 1878-81, Liverpool & District 1882-94, England 1880-88), D.Q. (Cambridge University 1876-79, Lancashire 1876-87, Liverpool & District 1882-86), E.E. (Lancashire 1884-1903, Liverpool & District 1887-93, Europeans 1892/93; Gentlemen of Liverpool 1884, Liverpool & District 1901-07 - not first-class), uncle of A.I. (Middlesex 1912). Lancashire (1883-96), Gentlemen of Liverpool (1884-89), Liverpool & District (1894-1904 - not first-class). rhb. rm. Club: Liverpool.

STUBBS, Thomas Alfred (1893-94) b West Derby, Liverpool, Lancashire 13.3.1872. Lancashire 2nd XI (1893), Liverpool & District (1894-95 - not first-class). Clubs: Sefton, Galveston USA.

SUGG, Frank Howe (1893-97) b Ilkeston, Derbyshire 11.1.1862. d Waterloo, Liverpool, Lancashire 29.5.1933. Brother of Walter (Yorkshire 1881, Derbyshire 1884-1902, Liverpool & District 1896-97 - not first-class). Yorkshire (1883), Derbyshire (1884-86), Lancashire (1887-99), England (1888, 2 Tests), Liverpool & District (1897 - not first-class). Soccer: Sheffield Wednesday, Derby County, Burnley. rhb. First-class Umpire 1926-27. Club: Wavertree.

THOMPSON, John Charles Peace (1892) b Chester, Cheshire 14.4.1870. d Tarset, Northumberland 31.12.1945. ed Harrow, Cambridge University. Cheshire (1892). Club: Chester Boughton Hall.

THOMPSON, William Henry (1892) b Padiham, Burnley, Lancashire 18.1.1866. d Southport, Lancashire 28.9.1920. ed Whalley GS. Clubs: Whalley, Padiham, Northern Great Crosby.

WATSON, Alexander (1882-84) b Coatbridge, Lanarkshire, Scotland 4.11.1844. d Old Trafford, Manchester, Lancashire 26.10.1920. Lancashire (1871-93), Cheshire (1876). rhb. rsr-a. Club: Manchester.

WHITE, John (1886-90) b Bulwell, Nottinghamshire 2.3.1855. North (1886), Nottinghamshire XI (1887). rhb. wk. Club: Liverpool.

WHITEHEAD, Stephen James (1891-92) b Enfield Highway, Middlesex 2.9.1860. d Small Heath, Birmingham, Warwickshire 9.6.1904. Warwickshire (1889-1900). rhb. rm. Club: Liverpool.

WOOD, Reginald (1884) b Woodchurch, Birkenhead, Cheshire 7.3.1860. d Manly, Sydney, New South Wales, Australia 6.1.1915. ed Charterhouse. Lancashire (1880-84), Victoria (1886/87), England (1886/87, 1 Test), Gentlemen of Liverpool (1884). Tour: to Australia 1886/87 - co-opted. lhb. lm. Club: Birkenhead Park.

WOODWARD, Edwin (1888-90) b Sutton-in-Ashfield, Nottinghamshire 17.9.1864. d Mansfield, Nottinghamshire 15.12.1953. Cheshire (1886-93). rhb. rm. Club: New Brighton.

YOUNG, William (1891) b Speedwell, Staveley, Derbyshire 8.3.1861. d Staveley, Derbyshire 6.10.1933. Derbyshire (1891). wk. Clubs: Sefton, Liverpool.

CRICKETERS WHO PLAYED FOR GENTLEMEN OF LIVERPOOL
(& DISTRICT) IN NON-FIRST-CLASS MATCHES

AINSLIE, Rev. Richard Montague (1889) b Easingwold, Yorkshire 23.1.1858. d Childwall, Liverpool, Lancashire 23.12.1924. ed St.Peter's York, Cambridge University. Club: Liverpool.

ASHWORTH, W. (1888) Club: Liverpool.

BARNES, William Pilkington (1911) b Liverpool, Lancashire 1870/1. d Aughton, Ormskirk, Lancashire 18.8.1931. Father of J.R. (Lancashire 1919-30, Liverpool & District 1920-32 - not first-class). Lancashire 2nd XI (1899-1906), Liverpool & District (1896-1907 - not first-class). Club: Ormskirk, Birkenhead Park.

BAUCHER, Frederick William (1906-20) b Wigan, Lancashire 6.11.1878. d Blundellsands, Liverpool, Lancashire 7.6.1947. Lancashire (1903), Liverpool & District (1906-20 - not first-class). rhb. wk. Club: Bootle.

BIRD, George (1884-89) b Crouch Hall, Hornsey, Middlesex 30.7.1849. d Esher, Surrey 28.10.1930. ed Highgate. Father of M.C. (Lancashire 1907, Surrey 1909-21, England 10 Tests) and A.C. (MCC 1914), brother of Walter (MCC 1880), grandfather of A.C. (Army in India 1933/34). Middlesex (1872-77), Lancashire (1880). rhb. wk. Club: Liverpool.

BLEASE, Harvey (1910) b West Derby, Liverpool, Lancashire 29.8.1882. d killed in action at Gallipoli, Dardenelles, Turkey 7.8.1915. ed Sedbergh. Liverpool & District (1906-07 - not first-class). rhb. Club: Sefton.

BOWRING, Frank Harvey (1910) b St.John's, Newfoundland, Canada 10.12.1878. d killed in action near St. Matin-sur-Cogeul, France 28.8.1918. ed Shrewsbury, Oxford University. Brother of William (Barbados 1899/00-1901/02, Gentlemen of Liverpool 1911). Liverpool & District (1901-03 - not first-class). Club: Liverpool.

BOWRING, William (1911) b St.John's, Newfoundland, Canada 14.11.1874. d Bay, St.Michael, Barbados 12.8.1945. ed Sherborne and Marlborough. Brother of F.H. (Gentlemen of Liverpool 1910, Liverpool & District 1901-03 - not first-class), brother-in-law of D.C.C.C.DaCosta (Barbados 1899/1900). Barbados (1899/00-1901/02). Tour: West Indies to England 1900 (not first-class). rhb. Club: Liverpool.

BRANCKER, Charles Henry (1888) b Mossley Hill, Liverpool, Lancashire 10.4.1858. d Copford Hall, near Colchester, Essex 17.5.1938. ed Marlborough. Club: Liverpool.

CHADWICK, Rev. Rohan Mackenzie (1910) b Bidston Hill, Birkenhead, Cheshire 11.9.1885. d Poole, Dorset 24.5.1968. ed Rugby. Cheshire (1909-10), Dorset. Club: Birkenhead Park.

CUNNINGHAM, James Cyril (1910-11) b Liverpool, Lancashire 22.7.1885. ed Rugby. Brother of Robert (Lancashire 2nd XI 1908, Gentlemen of Liverpool 1911, Liverpool & District 1920 - not first-class). Club: Liverpool.

CUNNINGHAM, Robert (1911) b Liverpool, Lancashire 25.2.1889. ed Rugby. Brother of J.C. (Gentlemen of Liverpool 1910-11). Lancashire 2nd XI (1908), Liverpool & District (1920 - not first-class). Club: Liverpool.

DUNLOP, Robert Gordon (1884) b Edinburgh, Scotland 14.7.1855. ed Edinburgh Academy. Club: Liverpool.

ECCLES, Alexander Percy (1888) b Huyton Park, Liverpool, Lancashire 11.1861. d Chester, Cheshire 14.6.1932. ed Uppingham, Cambridge University. Brother of Henry (Lancashire 1885-86, Liverpool & District 1889). Club: Huyton.

EVANS, Thomas (1887) - *see Liverpool & District first-class.*

FIELD, Samuel (1889) b Liverpool, Lancashire 5.1863. d 12.1897. ed Uppingham. Brother of George (Oxford University 1893). Club: Liverpool.

FRASER, Wallace (1911) b Bootle, Liverpool, Lancashire 30.11.1876. d killed in action near Guillemont, France 30.7.1916. ed Rugby. Secretary of Northern CC. Clubs: Liverpool, Northern Great Crosby.

HANNAY, Charles Scott (1910) b West Derby, Liverpool, Lancashire 2.11.1879. d Grassendale, Aigburth, Liverpool, Lancashire 27.6.1955. ed Rugby. Oxford University (1901), Liverpool & District (1903-07 - not first-class). rhb. rm. Club: Liverpool.

HOLDEN, Cecil (1887) - *see Liverpool & District first-class.*

HORNBY, Edgar Christian (1884-89) - *see Liverpool & District first-class.*

HORNBY, Gerald Frederick (1884) b Aigburth, Liverpool, Lancashire 9.6.1862. d Tarporley, Cheshire 9.2.1890. ed Winchester. Brother of E.C. (Lancashire 1885-87, Liverpool & District 1886-1901; Gentlemen of Liverpool 1884-89, Liverpool & District 1901 - not first-class) and Joseph (Gentlemen of Liverpool 1889), uncle of A.H. (Europeans 1934/35). Oxford University (1882). rhb. rf. Club: Liverpool.

HORNBY, Joseph (1889) b Huyton, Liverpool, Lancashire 9.2.1859. ed Winchester. Brother of E.C. (Lancashire 1885-87, Liverpool & District 1886-1901 Gentlemen of Liverpool 1884-89, Liverpool & District 1901 - not first-class) and G.F. (Oxford University 1882, Gentlemen of Liverpool 1884), uncle of A.H. (Europeans 1934/35). Clubs: Liverpool, Dingle.

JOHNSON, T. H. (1911)

JONES, Charles Langton (1887) - *see Liverpool & District first-class.*

JONES, F. (1887)

JONES, F. A. (1910) wk. Club: Birkenhead Park.

KEMBLE, Arthur Twiss (1887-89) - *see Liverpool & District first-class.*

KIRBY, Edmund Francis Joseph (1911) b Birkenhead, Cheshire 11.4.1874. ed Stoneyhurst. Cheshire (1911-12), Liverpool & District (1900-02 - not first-class). Club: Neston.

LEACH, Harold (1889) - *see Liverpool & District first-class.*

LOTT, Fred (1910) Club: Wavertree.

MANSON, E. (1884) Club: Liverpool.

MORRICE, Kenneth Digby Raikes (1910) b Birkenhead, Cheshire 4.8.1882. d Virginia Water, Surrey 7.9.1951. ed Brighton College. Cheshire (1909), Liverpool & District 1905-06 - not first-class). Club: Birkenhead Park.

NICHOLSON, George (1887-89) Club: Liverpool.

O'DWYER, James B. (1888-89) b St.Johns, Newfoundland, Canada 1865. Brother of William M.P. (Gentlemen of Liverpool 1888-89). Clubs: Liverpool, Dingle.

O'DWYER, William M. P. (1888-89) b St.Johns, Newfoundland, Canada 1863. Brother of James B. (Gentlemen of Liverpool 1888-89) Clubs: Liverpool, Dingle.

PARR, Henry Bingham (1884) b Grappenhall Heys, Cheshire 6.6.1845. d Liverpool 24.3.1930. ed Cheltenham. Brother of F.C. (Cheshire 1869-81, Hertfordshire) and T.P. (Cheshire 1873). Lancashire (1872-76), Cheshire (1874-78). rhb. Clubs: Liverpool, Birkenhead Park, Free Foresters.

POTTER, William Henry (1884) b Gufsey, India 20.8.1847. d Boreham Wood, Hertfordshire 10.4.1920. ed Hereford Cathedral School. Brother of T.O. (Lancashire 1866). Lancashire (1870), Herefordshire (1870-71). wk. Clubs: Liverpool, Birkenhead Park.

RATCLIFFE, Harold (1887) Brother of Edgar (Lancashire 1884, Liverpool & District 1886-89). wk. Club: Sefton.

RAVENSCROFT, James (1887) - *see Liverpool & District first-class.*

RIMMER, F. A. (1910-11) Lancashire 2nd XI (1908), Liverpool & District (1902-06 - not first-class). lfm. Club: Formby.

ROPER, Edward (1884-88) - *see Liverpool & District first-class.*

ROUGHTON, Lachesnez Ken (1888) b Kettering, Northamptonshire 10.1860. d 12.1901. ed Uppingham. Club: Liverpool.

SMITH, J. W. (1911) Club: Bootle.

STEEL, Ernest Eden (1884) - *see Liverpool & District first-class.*

STEEL, Harold Banner (1884-89) - *see Liverpool & District first-class.*

SWIFT, Rev. John McIntosh (1911) b Prescot, Lancashire 1.2.1886. d Bexhill-on-Sea, Sussex 25.4.1949. ed St.John's College, Cambridge University. Lancashire 2nd XI (1910), Cheshire (1911-13). Clubs: Prescot, Birkenhead Park.

WILLIAMS, Gerald Lloyd (1910) b Liverpool, Lancashire 28.8.1880. d Conway, Caernarvonshire 1Q, 1936. ed Sedbergh. Rugby Union: Lancashire, Anglo-Welsh tour of Australia and New Zealand. Clubs: Sefton, Oxton.

WOOD, Reginald (1884) - *see Liverpool & District first-class.*

CRICKETERS WHO PLAYED FOR LIVERPOOL & DISTRICT IN NON-FIRST-CLASS MATCHES

ADAMS, Lionel Bertram Paddock ("Bill") (1947) b West Derby, Liverpool, Lancashire 9.9.1914. d Hightown, Merseyside 11.5.1991. ed Merchant Taylors, Crosby. Lancashire 2nd XI (1939-49), Sussex XI (1943), Navy (1943), Cheshire (1953-55). rhb. Club: Hightown.

AINSCOUGH, Hugh ("Hugo") (1894) b Parbold, Lancashire 3.1.1860. d Formby, Lancashire 31.5.1945. ed Ampleforth. Brother of John (Liverpool & District 1895) and Thomas (Liverpool & District 1891-1894, Lancashire 1894-1906, Liverpool & District 1894-1904 - not first-class). wk. Club: Ormskirk.

AINSCOUGH, John (1895) b New House, Parbold Mill, Lancashire 5.6.1863. d Briars Hall, Lathom, Lancashire 3.8.1937. ed Ampleforth. Brother of Hugh (Liverpool & District 1894) and Thomas (Liverpool & District 1891-1894, Lancashire 1894-1906, Liverpool & District 1894-1904 - not first-class). Club: Ormskirk.

AINSCOUGH, Thomas (1894-1904) - *see Liverpool & District first-class*.

AINSWORTH, Jerry Lionel (1896) b Freshfield, Formby, Lancashire 11.9.1877. d Falmouth, Cornwall 30.12.1923. ed Marlborough. Brother of G.W.B. (Leveson-Gower's XI 1902). Lancashire (1899), Europeans (1904/05). Tour: to North America 1898. lhb. sla. Clubs: Liverpool, Formby.

ALLEN, Wilfred Gordon (1947) b South Elmsett, Yorkshire 13.3 1913. d Wallasey, Cheshire 9.2.1983. ed Wakefield GS, Cambridge University. Cheshire (1947-56). rhb. wk. Clubs: Oxton, New Brighton.

ASHCROFT, Edward (1947) b Aughton, Ormskirk, Lancashire 22.12.1912. d Aughton, Ormskirk, Lancashire 8.12.1975. ed Ormskirk GS. Club: Ormskirk.

BARDSWELL, Gerald Roscoe (1894-1902) b Woolton, Liverpool, Lancashire 7.12.1873. d New Orleans, Louisiana, USA 29.12.1906. ed Uppingham. Lancashire (1894-1902), Oxford University (1894-97). Tours: to North America 1894, to West Indies 1896/97. rhb. rm. Club: Formby.

BARNES, John Reginald (1920-32) b Aughton, Ormskirk, Lancashire 18.5.1897. d Grange-over-Sands, Lancashire 22.7.1945. ed Marlborough. Son of W.P. (Liverpool & District 1896-1907 - not first-class, Gentlemen of Liverpool 1911, Lancashire 2nd XI 1899-1906). Lancashire (1919-30). rhb. rlb. Clubs: Ormskirk, Liverpool.

BARNES, William Pilkington (1896-1907) - see *Gentlemen of Liverpool (& District)*.

BARRELL, Ben (1932) b Orford, Suffolk 14.5.1885. d Bootle, Liverpool 14.7.1969. Lancashire (1911-23), Cheshire (1913). rhb. rfm. Clubs: Crompton, Huyton.

BATES, William Frederick (1932) b Kirkheaton, Yorkshire 5.3.1884. d Belfast, Northern Ireland 17.1.1957. Son of Willie (Yorkshire 1877-87, England 15 Tests). Yorkshire (1907-13), Glamorgan (1921-31), Wales (1923-30), Cheshire (1933-36). rhb. sla. Club: Neston.

BAUCHER, Frederick William (1906-20) - see *Gentlemen of Liverpool (& District)*.

BLACKBURN, William Edward (1920) b Clitheroe, Lancashire 24.11.1888. d Heaton, Bolton, Lancashire 3.6.1941. Yorkshire (1919-20). rhb. rfm. Club: Liverpool, Hightown.

BLEASE, Harvey (1906-07) - *see Gentlemen of Liverpool (& District)*.

BOSWELL, Arthur Hedley (1904-05) b Toxteth Park, Liverpool, Lancashire 2Q, 1872. lb. Club: Sefton.

BOUMPHREY, Donald (1920) b Birkenhead, Cheshire 4.10.1892. d Holt Green, Aughton, Ormskirk, Lancashire 12.9.1971. ed Shrewsbury. Brother of Colin (R.A.F. 1932, Cheshire 1920-26). Wales (1928), Cheshire (1914-33), Denbighshire. rhb. Club: Wallasey.

BOWRING, Frank Harvey (1901-03) - *see Gentlemen of Liverpool (& District)*.

BRETHERTON, James (1895-98) - *see Liverpool & District first-class*.

BROCK, Arthur William (1904) b Liverpool, Lancashire 2Q, 1871. wk. Club: Sefton.

BROCKLEBANK, Ernest (1905) b Oxton, Birkenhead, Cheshire 4Q, 1873. Cheshire (1910). Club: Birkenhead Victoria.

BROCKLEBANK, Sir John Montague (1947) b Hoylake, Cheshire 3.9.1915. d Palazz Zetjun, Malta 13.9.1974. ed Eton. Brother of Sir T.A.L. (Cambridge University 1919, Cheshire 1921), nephew of Sir F.S.Jackson (England 1893-1905, Yorkshire 1890-1907, Cambridge University 1890-93). Cambridge University (1936), Lancashire (1939), Bengal (1947/48). rhb. rlb. Tours: to Canada 1937, selected for the cancelled tour to India 1939/40. Club: Liverpool.

BROWN, Harry Stewart (1932) b c1897. d Bebington, Wirral, Cheshire 7.3.1984. A member of the Cheshire CCC Committee for over 30 years. rhb. wk. Club: Bootle.

BROWN, Joseph Henry (1904-07) b Earl Shilton, Leicestershire 26.1.1872. d Earl Shilton, Leicestershire 27.4.1915. Brother of Lewis (Leicestershire 1896-1903). Leicestershire (1898-1905). rhb. rob. Clubs: Birkenhead Park, Sefton, Colne.

BURROUGH, Rev. John (1900-02) b Clun, Shropshire 5.7.1873. d St.Leonards-on-Sea, Sussex 26.12.1922. ed King's, Bruton and Shrewsbury. Brother of W.G. (Somerset 1906), uncle of H.D. (Somerset 1927-47) and Rev.J.W. (Oxford University 1924-26, Gloucestershire 1924-37). Herefordshire (1890), Cambridge University (1893-95), Free Foresters (1914). rhb. rfm. Clubs: Northern Waterloo, Huyton.

COLE, Terence George Owen (1901-03) b Llanrhaiadr, Denbighshire 14.11.1877. d Stoke Court, near Taunton, Somerset 15.12.1944. ed Harrow. Cambridge University (1898), Lancashire (1904), Derbyshire (1913), Somerset (1922), Denbighshire (1905). Tour: to West Indies 1904/05. rhb. sla. Club: Liverpool.

COURT, Leonard (1906) b Tranmere, Birkenhead, Cheshire 3Q, 1876. Brother of Morris (Cheshire 1895). Cheshire (1909). rhb. rfm. Club: Oxton.

CROSFIELD, Sydney Morland (1895) - *see Liverpool & District first-class.*

CUNNINGHAM, Robert (1920) - *see Gentlemen of Liverpool (& District).*

DUCKHAM, Walter (1932) b Coventry, Warwickshire 16.1.1906. d Ipswich Hospital, Suffolk 16.9.1984. Warwickshire 2nd XI (1928), Suffolk (1946-53). rhb. rm. Club: Formby.

GARNETT, Harold Gwyer (1899-1905) b Aigburth, Liverpool, Lancashire 19.11.1879. d killed in action at Matcoing, Cambrai, France 3.12.1917. ed Clifton. Brother of F.M. (Europeans 1917/18-1921/22). Lancashire (1899-1914), Argentine (1911/12). lhb. sla. Tours: to Australia 1901/02. Club: Liverpool.

GOODWIN, Francis Herbert (1899) b Rainhill, Lancashire 4.1.1866. d Garston, Liverpool, Lancashire 20.1.1931. Lancashire (1894). lhb. sla. Clubs: Liverpool, St.Helens.

GRAHAM, Allan James (1906) b Liverpool, Lancashire 16.5.1883. d Hoylake, Cheshire 27.6.1941. ed Marlborough, Oxford University. O.B.E. 1919, C.B.E. 1920. Golf: England 1908. Club: Liverpool.

GRAYSON, John Hubert FitzHenry (1895) - *see Liverpool & District first-class.*

GREENHALGH, Eric Washington (1947) b Sale, Cheshire 18.5.1910. d Wirral, Cheshire 2.7.1996. Lancashire (1935-38). rhb. rm. Club: Liverpool.

GREGORY, James Clark (1900-04) b Sutton-in-Ashfield, Nottinghamshire 2Q, 1870. Nottinghamshire Colts (1890). Clubs: Liverpool, Huyton.

GREWCOCK, George (1902) b Barwell, Leicestershire 16.5.1862. d Toxteth Park, Liverpool, Lancashire 15.8.1922. Leicestershire (1899). lhb. lfm. Clubs: Sefton, New Brighton.

HAMPSHIRE, George Newton (1904-05) b Liverpool, Lancashire 19.3.1877. ed Rossall. wk. Club: Liverpool.

HANCOCK, Harry Bentley (1903-07) b Birkenhead, Cheshire 4Q, 1874. d Birkenhead, Cheshire 8.8.1923. Cheshire (1909). Club: Oxton.

HANDFORD, Alick (1894) - *see Liverpool & District first-class.*

HANNAY, Charles Scott (1903-07) - *see Gentlemen of Liverpool (& District).*

HENSON, Richard (1898) - *see Liverpool & District first-class.*

HICKMOTT, William Edward (1932) b Boxley, Kent 10.4.1893. d West Malling, Kent 16.1.1968. Nephew of Edward (Kent 1875-88). Kent (1914-21), Lancashire (1923-24). rhb. lsm. Club: Wallasey.

HILTON, W. H. (1894-96) Clubs: Liverpool, Dingle.

HODGSON, Herbert William (1920-32) b Toxteth Park, Liverpool, Lancashire 23.5.1891. d Sewardstonebury, Chelmsford, Essex 30.4.1964. Brother of J.P. (Cheshire 1921-32). Cheshire (1914-32), Minor Counties (1924-27). rhb. rf. Clubs: Rock Ferry, Birkenhead Park.

HOLDEN, Cecil (1895-1901) - *see Liverpool & District first-class.*

18

HOME, Harry (1894) Flintshire (1886). lhb. rm. Club: Ormskirk.

HORNBY, Edgar Christian (1901) - *see Liverpool & District first-class.*

HOWARD, Dr. W. (1932) Club: Southport & Birkdale.

HUBBACK, Theodore Rathbone (1895) - *see Liverpool & District first-class.*

HUTTON, Charles Frederick (1896-98) b Oxton, Birkenhead, Cheshire 20.12.1868. d Exmouth, Devon 9.5.1938. ed Harrow. Son of A. (Lancashire 1851). Cheshire (1892-93). Club: Oxton.

JOHNSON, E. F. H. (1920)

JOHNSTON, J. Dudley (1900-01) b Liverpool, Lancashire 1869. ed Cambridge House, Litherland. Club: Huyton, Stoneycroft.

KEMBLE, Arthur Twiss (1894-1903) - *see Liverpool & District first-class.*

KING, John Herbert (1897) b Lutterworth, Leicestershire 16.4.1871. d Denbigh, North Wales 18.11.1946. Brother of James (Leicestershire 1899-1905), uncle of J.W. (Worcestershire 1927-28, Leicestershire 1929). Leicestershire (1895-1925), England (1 Test). lhb. lm. Club: Birkenhead Park.

KIRBY, Edmund Francis Joseph (1900-02) - *see Gentlemen of Liverpool (& District).*

KITCHENER, Frederick George (1901-05) b Hartley Row, Hampshire 2.7.1871. d East Boldon, Durham 25.5.1948. Hampshire (1896-1903). rhb. rfm. Club: Ormskirk, Sefton.

LASHMAR, John William Turner (1898) b Godstone, Surrey c1863/4. d Great Crosby, Liverpool, Lancashire 27.1.1910. Club: Northern Great Crosby.

LEACH, Harold (1898) - *see Liverpool & District first-class.*

LEATHER, Arthur Bowring (1901-03) b Garston, Liverpool, Lancashire 17.10.1879. ed Shrewsbury. Club: Liverpool.

LEGARD, Antony Ronald (1947) b Sialkot, India 17.1.1912. ed Winchester. Oxford University (1932-35), Worcestershire (1935), Europeans (1943/44), MCC (1952). rhb. rm. Club: Liverpool.

LISTER, William Hubert Lionel (1947) b Freshfield, Formby, Lancashire 11.10.1911. d Bridgnorth, Shropshire 29.7.1998. ed Malvern. Cambridge University (1933), Lancashire (1933-39). rhb. Club: Formby.

LORRIMER, D. A. (1894) Clubs: Birkenhead Park, Oxton.

McCORMICK, Rev. Joseph Gough (1906) b New Cross, London 19.2.1874. d Higher Broughton, Manchester, Lancashire 30.8.1924. ed Exeter and Cambridge University. Son of Rev. Joseph (Cambridge University 1854-56, MCC, Ireland 1855-58). Devon (1893-). Kent 2nd XI (1895), Norfolk (1899-1909), I Zingari. rhb. srh. Club: Liverpool.

McENTYRE, Douglas Percival (1920) b Wallasey, Cheshire 30.1.1899. d Beckenham, Kent 2.1874. Brother of A.L. (Cheshire 1935-47), G.A. (Cheshire 1929-46, Liverpool & District 1947 - not first-class), J.A. (Cheshire 1928-36) and K.H. (Cheshire 1927-38), uncle of C.G. (Cheshire 1970) and K.B. (Surrey 1965-66, Cheshire 1962-68). Cheshire (1920-27). rhb. Club: Liverpool.

McENTYRE, George Austen (1947) b Wallasey, Cheshire 23.12.1910. d Warrington, Lancashire 26.11.1975. ed Elleray Park. Brother of A.L. (Cheshire 1935-47), D.P. (Cheshire 1920-27, Liverpool & District 1920 - not first-class), J.A. (Cheshire 1928-36) and K.H. (Cheshire 1927-38), father of C.G. (Cheshire 1970) and K.B. (Surrey 1965-66, Cheshire 1962-68). Cheshire (1929-46). rhb. Clubs: Wallasey, Oxton.

McLEOD, Kenneth Grant (1920) b Liverpool, Lancashire 2.2.1888. d St.James, Cape Province, South Africa 7.3.1967. ed Fettes. Cambridge University (1908-09), Lancashire (1908-13), Free Foresters (1914). Rugby: Cambridge University and Scotland. rhb. rf. Club: Liverpool.

MAKEPEACE, Joseph William Henry (Harry) (1907) b Middlesborough, Yorkshire 22.8.1881. d Spital, Bebington, Cheshire 19.12.1952. Lancashire (1906-30), England (4 Tests). Tour: to Australia 1920/21. Soccer: Everton and England. rhb. rlb. Club: Liverpool.

MASON, Percy (1902-07) b East Bridgford, Nottinghamshire 19.11.1873. d Gunthorpe, Nottinghamshire 27.11.1952. Nottinghamshire (1896-1901), Cheshire (1909-12). rhb. rf. Club: Bootle.

MORRICE, Kenneth Digby Raikes (1905-06) - *see Gentlemen of Liverpool (& District).*

NEEDHAM, Elijah (1898) b Loughborough, Leicestershire 4Q, 1866. d Shepshed, Leicestershire 14.12.1929. Leicestershire (1890), Cheshire (1894). Clubs: Bootle, Rock Ferry.

NICHOLAS, Frederick William Herbert (1932) b Federated Malay States 25.7.1893. d Kensington, London 20.10.1962. ed Forest and Oxford University. Grandfather of M.C.J. (Hampshire 1978-95). Essex (1912-29), Bedfordshire (1913). Tours: to South Africa 1924/25, to Jamaica 1928/29, to Argentina 1929/30. rhb. wk. Club: Liverpool.

NUTTER, Albert Edward (1932) b Burnley, Lancashire 28.6.1913. d Cape Town, South Africa 3.6.1996. Lancashire (1935-45), Northamptonshire (1948-53). rhb. rfm. Club: Formby.

OAKLEY, William (1895-97) - *see Liverpool & District first-class.*

O'HARA, Dr. W. E. (1905) Clubs: Liverpool, Dingle.

PEEL, Lionel George (1901) b Rock Ferry, Wirral, Cheshire 13.10.1873. Club: Rock Ferry.

PILKINGTON, Charles Carlisle (1899) b Woolton, Liverpool, Lancashire 13.12.1876. d South Warnborough Manor, Hampshire 8.1.1950. ed Eton. Brother of H.C. (Oxford University 1899-1900, Middlesex 1903-04, Liverpool & District 1900 - not first-class), father of T.A. (MCC to South America). Lancashire (1895), Oxford University (1896), Middlesex (1903), Gentlemen of England (1919). rhb. rm. Club: Liverpool.

PILKINGTON, Hubert Carlisle (1900) b Woolton, Liverpool, Lancashire 23.10.1879. d Letchworth, Hertfordshire 17.6.1942. ed Eton. Brother of C.C. (Lancashire 1895, Oxford University 1896, Middlesex 1903, Liverpool & District 1899 - not first-class), uncle of T.A. (MCC to South America), son-in-law of C.F.H.Leslie (Oxford University 1881-83, Middlesex 1881-86, England 4 Tests), brother-in-law of J.Leslie (Oxford University 1908). Oxford University (1899-1900), Middlesex (1903-04). rhb. ras. Club: Liverpool.

PRICE, William (1896) - *see Liverpool & District first-class.*

RAPKIN, Lt-Cdr. Geoffrey Jennings O.B.E. (1920) b Sidcup, Kent 1Q, 1883. Clubs: Huyton, Liverpool.

RIMMER, F. A. (1902-06) - *see Gentlemen of Liverpool (& District).*

RINGROSE, William (1895-1900) b Manston, Yorkshire 2.9.1871. d Cross Gates. Leeds, Yorkshire 14.9.1943. Yorkshire (1901-06), Scotland (1908-12). Yorkshire scorer (1923-39). lhb. rfm. Club: Liverpool.

SHARP, John ("Jack") (1895) b Hereford, Herefordshire 15.1.1878. d Wavertree, Liverpool, Lancashire 28.1.1938. rhb. lfm. Lancashire (1899-1925), England (3 Tests), Herefordshire. Soccer: Aston Villa, Everton and England. Club: Liverpool.

SHEPHERD, Sydney George (1947) b York, Yorkshire 23.8.1908. d Craigadwywynt, Ruthin, Denbighshire, Wales 20.12.1987. Worcestershire (1936), Cheshire (1946-59). rhb rfm. Club: Bootle.

SHUTT, Thomas (1901) b Burnley, Lancashire Club: Northern Waterloo.

SMITH, Albert (1894-95) - *see Liverpool & District first-class.*

SPOONER, Archibald Franklin (1904-06) b Litherland, Liverpool, Lancashire 21.5.1886. d Dartmouth, Devon 11.1.1965. ed Haileybury. Brother of R.H. (Lancashire 1899-1921, England 1905-10, 10 Tests; Liverpool & District 1903 - not first-class). Lancashire (1906-09). rhb. Club: Liverpool.

SPOONER, Reginald Herbert (1903) b Litherland, Liverpool, Lancashire 21.10.1880. d Lincoln 2.10.1961. ed Marlborough. Brother of A.F. (Lancashire 1906-09, Liverpool & District 1904-06 - not first-class). Lancashire (1899-1921), England (10 Tests). Rugby: Lancashire and England. rhb. sra. Club: Liverpool.

STEEL, Ernest Eden (1901-07) - *see Liverpool & District first-class.*

STEEL, Harold Banner (1894-1904) - *see Liverpool & District first-class.*

STODDART, Wilfred Bowring (1896-1920) b West Derby, Liverpool, Lancashire 27.4.1871. d Wood End Park, Grassendale, Liverpool, Lancashire 8.1.1935. ed Liverpool Institute. Lancashire (1898-99), Rugby: Lancashire and England. rhb. rlb. Clubs: Liverpool, Dingle.

STOTT, Alfred (1899-1904) b New Ferry, Birkenhead, Cheshire 1871. Cheshire (1892), Lancashire 2nd XI (1900). rhb. rf. Clubs: Rock Ferry, Liverpool.

STUBBS, Thomas Alfred (1894-95) - *see Liverpool & District first-class.*

SUGG, Frank Howe (1897) - *see Liverpool & District first-class.*

SUGG, Walter (1896-97) b Ilkeston, Derbyshire 21.5.1860. d Dore, Yorkshire 21.5.1933. Brother of F.H. (Yorkshire 1883, Derbyshire 1884-86, Lancashire 1887-99, England 1888, 2 Tests, Liverpool & District 1893, Liverpool & District 1897 - not first-class). Yorkshire (1881), Derbyshire (1884-1902). rhb. rm. Clubs: Ormskirk, Bootle.

TAYLOR, Robert Hall M. (1903-07) b Birkenhead, Cheshire 3Q, 1876. rhb. Club: Oxton.

THOMPSON, Frank Gledhill (1901-05) b Birkenhead, Cheshire 1.10.1874. d Blundellsands, Liverpool, Lancashire 11.8.1933. ed Merchant Taylors, Crosby. Clubs: Northern Waterloo and Great Crosby.

TYLER, Ray (1947) b Ridlington, Rutland 26.10.1922. Son of Bernard (Northamptonshire 1923-24, Leicestershire 1926-28). Lancashire 2nd XI (1948). rhb. Club: Liverpool.

WARLOW, Charles Arthur (1932) b Ormskirk, Lancashire 6.3.1907. d Tissington, Derbyshire, 22.10.1997. ed Ormskirk GS. Son of C.M. (Liverpool & District 1904 - not first-class). rhb. Club: Ormskirk.

WARLOW, Charles Medcalf (1904) b Ormskirk, Lancashire 18.6.1872. d Parwich Hospital, Bakewell, Derbyshire 6.5.1947. ed Ormskirk GS. Father of C.A. (Liverpool & District 1932 - not first-class). rhb. Club: Ormskirk.

WARREN, Arnold (R.) (1901) b Codnor Park, Derbyshire 2.4.1875. d Codnor, Derbyshire 3.9.1951. Derbyshire (1897-1920), England (1905, 1 Test). First-class Umpire (1923-26). rhb. rfm. Soccer: Derby County. Club: Birkdale.

WEAVER, F. W. H. (1904) Club: Liverpool.

WILSON, Charles Elliott (1905) b Blackheath, Kent 10.1879. d 10.1941. ed Uppingham. Club: Huyton.

WOLSTENHOLME, Arthur Mellor (1947) b Leominster, Herefordshire 8.8.1915. d Claughton, Birkenhead, Cheshire 3.10.1990. ed Leominster GS. Cheshire (1935-52). rhb. Club: Oxton.

BIBLIOGRAPHY

2208   The Complete History of Liverpool & District (including Gentlemen of Liverpool) versus Colonial and Foreign Teams, First-class Counties and Cambridge University. Compiled by George A.Brooking. Liverpool, 1931. 84p.

7383   55 Years Cricket Memories. By George A.Brooking. Liverpool, 1948. 156p.

2209   Liverpool [and District] Cricket Annual. 1889 (3rd issue)-1890, 1926-1931, 1950-1965. Liverpool, W.Blevin.

2164   Merseyside Cricket Handbook. 1926-1928. Edited by J.MacDowall. Liverpool, J.MacDowall.

1113   Liverpool & District Cricket Competition. Official Handbook. 1986-1987, 1989-2001.

1111   The Liverpool Competition: a study of the development of cricket on Merseyside. By Peter N.Walker. Birkenhead, 1988. 87p.

-       Cheshire Cricketers 1822-1996. Compiled by Tony Percival. West Bridgford, ACS, 1997. 80p.

1140   Lancashire Cricketers 1865-1988. [includes Liverpool & District Cricketers] Compiled by Malcolm Lorimer. West Bridgford, ACS, 1989. 50p.

-       Cricket Grounds of Lancashire. By Malcolm Lorimer and Don Ambrose. West Bridgford, ACS, 1992. 72p.

806   Birkenhead Park. By Jean McInnes. Birkenhead, 1984. 61p.

-       Birkenhead Park Cricket Club 1846-1996. By Chris Elston. Prenton, 1997. 48p.

1092   Bootle Cricket Club. Souvenir Handbook. Seasons 1948-1950. Bootle, 1950. 16p.

1094   Bootle Cricket Club. 150th Anniversary 1833-1983. Souvenir Book. Edited by P.C.Massen. Bootle, 1983. 72p.

1797-3 A century at Boughton Hall, A History of Chester Boughton Hall CC. 1873-1973. By Alan Robinson. Chester, 1973. 38p.

-       The Story of Garston and its Church. (includes Garston Cricket Club p.218). By Rev.J.M.Swift. Garston, 1937. 232p.

2202   Huyton Cricket and Bowling Club. Centenary Souvenir Programme 1860-1960. Huyton, 1960. 36p.

2210   Liverpool Cricket Club. Matches 1847-1864. Liverpool, 1865. 254p.

2211   L.C.C. Public School Tours, 1866 to 1896, also Birkenhead Park 1865 to 1896. Liverpool, 1896. 142p.
        - 1866 to 1907. Liverpool, 1907. 144p.
        - 1866 to 1912. Liverpool, 1912. 179p.

2212   Liverpool Cricket Club: A sketch of the historic continuity of the club. Local champions - Season 1919. By P.Y.Lodge. Liverpool, 1920. 16p.

2213   A Sketch of the Liverpool Cricket Club. [contains the rules of the Mosslake Field Cricket Society 1807]. Liverpool, 1930. 4p.

-       Liverpool Cricket Club. Souvenir Brochure of Lancashire v Kent, 26-29 June 2002 and Lancashire v West Indies 'A' 11-13 July 2002. [contains a short history of the club by John Wylie and an article on 'The Tyler Connection'.]

1805   Fifty years of Neston Cricket. By J.H.Gilling. Neston, 1947. 72p.

1096   History of the Northern Cricket Club. 1859-1961. By David C.Price. Crosby, 1985. 81p.

1117   Ormskirk Cricket Club 1835-1935. By Walter Stretch. Ormskirk, 1935. 32p.

1116   Ormskirk Cricket Club 1835-1985. 150 Not Out. Ormskirk, 1985. 52p.

1805-1 Oxton Cricket Club 1875-1975. Oxton, 1975. 20p.

2216   Sefton Cricket Club. 1862-1925. By J.D.Lynch. Liverpool, 1926. 44p.

2217   A Sportsman's Memories. By Edward Roper, edited by F.W.Wood. Liverpool, 1921. 286p.

2218   Sefton Cricket Club. Centenary Souvenir Programme. 1860-1960. Liverpool, 1960. 40p.

2247-1 [Southport & Birkdale Cricket Club]. A Hundred Years of Cricket at Trafalgar Road. 1874-1974. By Keith H.Porter. Southport, 1974. 44p.

1808   Wallasey Cricket Club, 1864-1964. Centenary Souvenir Brochure. By H.A.Wolfe. Wallasey, 1964. 32p.

2219   History of Waterloo Park Cricket Club 1890 - 1950: a Diamond Jubilee Souvenir. By Jack Matthews and Frederick B.Davidson. Liverpool, 1951. 74p.

-       Wavertree Cricket Club. Centenary 1854-1954. by R.J.Owen and W.H.Weights. Liverpool, 1954. 24p.

2249   Widnes Cricket Club. A souvenir of the club's 50 years at Lowerhouse Lane 1874-1924. Garston, 1924. 57p.

1129   Widnes Cricket Club. Centenary Year: 1865-1965. Widnes, 1965.

Both the Liverpool and the Birkenhead Park clubs hold large collections of minute books and score-books going back to the 1860s. The original scorebook of the Liverpool Cricket Club for 1822 and 1823 is in a private collection but the club holds a photocopy of a manuscript copy.

The reference library at Huyton holds the original minute book of the Huyton Cricket Club 1860-63 and the scrapbooks of the Rev.O.Penrhyn (1882-92), Tom Stone (1899-1936) and Harry Owen (1936-80). They can be viewed subject to prior permission from the club.

The Lancashire Country Cricket Club, Old Trafford, Library holds two scrapbooks of A.T.Kemble (1891-1900).

The number before each entry is the Padwick reference number.

LIVERPOOL & DISTRICT RECORDS IN FIRST-CLASS MATCHES

All matches were played at Aigburth

Played – 14. Won – 3. Lost – 8. Drawn – 3.

Highest Innings Total	For	269		v Yorkshire	1891
	Against	354		for Yorkshire	1892
Lowest Innings Total	For	45		v Yorkshire	1889
	Against	69		for Yorkshire	1892
Highest Individual Innings					
	For	100	A.G.Steel	v Yorkshire	1891
	Against	141	J.T.Brown	for Yorkshire	1894
Best Bowling in an Innings					
	For	7-46	H.Richardson	v Australians	1888
	Against	7-24	R.W.McLeod	for Australians	1893
Best Bowling in a Match	For	11-70	J.Crossland	v Australians	1884
	Against	12-77	R.Peel	for Yorkshire	1889

Best Partnerships - For

1	50	A.G.Steel and A.C.MacLaren	v Yorkshire	1892
2	108	A.G.Steel and H.Leach	v Yorkshire	1891
3	114	A.C.MacLaren and T.Ainscough	v Yorkshire	1892
4	61	A.G.Steel and E.Ratcliffe	v Australians	1886
5	81	C.Holden and J.H.F.Grayson	v Yorkshire	1891
6	26	T.Ainscough and E.Smith	v Yorkshire	1894
7	29	A.G.Steel and A.Champion	v Yorkshire	1889
8	75	E.C.Hornby and C.Shore	v Australians	1886
9	88	H.Richardson and C.Shore	v Yorkshire	1887
10	25	A.Price and F.J.Jones	v Yorkshire	1889

Best Partnerships - Against

1	70	L.Hall and G.Ulyett	for Yorkshire	1890
2	183	T.A.Wardall and L.Hall	for Yorkshire	1892
3	121	G.Ulyett and F.Lee	for Yorkshire	1889
4	73	G.Ulyett and W.Cartman	for Yorkshire	1891
5	115	T.P.Horan and G.Giffen	for Australians	1882
6	69	W.L.Murdoch and J.M.Blackham	for Australians	1884
7	72	R.W.Frank and G.Ulyett	for Yorkshire	1893
8	75	R.W.Frank and J.T.Brown	for Yorkshire	1893
9	52	S.Wade and J.Hunter	for Yorkshire	1890
10	121	J.T.Brown and D.Hunter	for Yorkshire	1894

LIVERPOOL & DISTRICT
RECORDS IN NON-FIRST-CLASS MATCHES

All matches were played at Aigburth

Played – 24. Won – 7. Lost – 11. Drawn – 6.

Highest Innings Total	For	421	v G.L.Jessop's Gloucestershire XI	1901
	Against	431	for Cambridge University	1900
Lowest Innings Total	For	47	v Cambridge University	1895
	Against	71	for Cambridge University	1896
Highest Individual Innings				
	For	195	T.Ainscough	
			v G.L.Jessop's Gloucestershire XI	1901
	Against	163	N.F.Druce	
			for Cambridge University	1897
Best Bowling in an Innings				
	For	8-42	J.Bretherton v Yorkshire	1895
	Against	9-120	E.M.Dowson	
			for Cambridge University	1901
Best Bowling in a Match	For	16-115	W.Ringrose v Cambridge University	1896
	Against	13-98	C.E.M.Wilson	
			for Cambridge University	1897

Best Partnerships - For

1	118	H.W.Hodgson and W.E.Bates	v South Americans	1932
2	150	T.Ainscough and H.G.Garnett	v G.L.Jessop's Gloucestershire XI	1901
3	124	H.G.Garnett and W.P.Barnes	v Cambridge University	1900
4	164*	K.D.R.Morrice and C.E.Wilson	v Cambridge University	1907
5	96	T.Ainscough and W.P.Barnes	v G.L.Jessop's Gloucestershire XI	1902
6	117	E.C.Hornby and A.B.Leather	v G.L.Jessop's Gloucestershire XI	1901
7	88	W.P.Barnes and J.H.King	v Cambridge University	1906
8	80	W.P.Barnes and F.W.Baucher	v Cambridge University	1906
9	56	W.P.Barnes and W.B.Stoddart	v Cambridge University	1900
10	45	W.Hilton and W.Ringrose	v Yorkshire	1895

Best Partnerships - Against

1	198	D.Ayling and A.L.S.Jackson	for South Americans	1932
2	123	D.Ayling and R.Stuart	for South Americans	1932
3	189	N.F.Druce and S.H.Day	for Cambridge University	1900
4	146	L.C.Braund and A.E.Lewis	for S.M.J.Woods' Somerset XI	1903
5	136	F.Mitchell and H.H.Marriott	for Cambridge University	1895
6	221	R.A.Young and F.H.Mugliston	for Cambridge University	1906
7	133	G.L.Jessop and N.O.Tagart	for G.L.Jessop's Gloucestershire XI	
				1901
8	123	R.W.Frank and T.W.Foster	for Yorkshire	1895
9	77	W.G.Druce and J.Burrough	for Cambridge University	1895
10	98	H.C.McDonnell and G.M.Buckston	for Cambridge University	1903

LIVERPOOL & DISTRICT FIRST-CLASS CAREER RECORDS

Name	First	Last	M	I	NO	Runs	HS	Avg	100	Runs	Wkts	OW	Avg	Best	5i	10m	ct	st
Ainscough, T.	1891	1894	3	6	1	154	61*	30.80		79	4		19.75	2/28			2	
Aspinall, F.	1891	1906	5	9	1	194	61*	24.25									3	
	1892		1	2	1	27	16	27.00									2	
	1882	1884	2	4	0	66	24	16.50									2	
Barlow, R.G.	1871	1891	351	608	64	11217	117	20.61	4	13799	950		14.52	9/39	66	14	268	2
	1890	1894	6	11	1	165	50	16.50		396	24		16.50	5/30	1		2	
Bretherton, J.	1882	1884	2	4	1	40	23	13.33		31	0							
Briggs, J.	1879	1900	535	826	55	14092	186	18.27	10	35430	2221		15.95	10/55	200	52	258	1
Brutton, Rev. E.B.	1892		1	2	0	15	12	7.50		29	0						1	
Chambers, C.G.	1885	1892	2	4	1	33	18*	11.00		37	0						1	
Champion, A.	1894		1	2	0	21	16	10.50		13	0							
	1889	1890	3	6	0	66	28	11.00									1	
Chapman, M.	1876	1890	18	31	4	218	29	8.07		17	1		17.00	1/10			9	
	1893		1	2	0	38	23	19.00										
	1884	1895	28	54	6	633	56	13.18		30	0						21	
Cox, G.R.	1890		1	2	0	0	0	0.00		3	0							
	1883	1899	1	2	0	46	27	23.00										
Crosfield, S.M.	1882	1884	96	150	14	2027	82*	14.90		151	3		50.33	1/1			49	
	1878	1887	2	4	0	5	3	1.25		142	18		7.88	7/72	3	1		
Crossland, J.	1894		84	132	25	1172	51	10.95		4019	322		12.48	8/57	25	6	32	
Disney, J.J.	1881	1894	1	2	0	1	1	1.00										
Dobell, P.	1886	1888	57	101	30	377	27*	5.30									97	12
Durandu, A.	1886	1888	3	5	1	46	25	11.50									3	
Eccles, H.	1887		10	17	2	142	28	9.46									4	
Evans, T.	1889		1	2	0	0	0	0.00									2	
	1885	1889	2	3	0	5	5	1.66									2	
	1886	1889	1	2	1	3	3*	3.00									1	
Fieldwick, E.	1883	1889	6	9	1	40	14	5.00		59	3		19.66	2/27			1	
	1894		2	3	0	13	10	4.33									2	
Grayson, H.M.	1889	1890	4	7	0	91	35	13.00		150	6		25.00	2/27			2	
Grayson, J.H.F.	1891	1893	1	2	0	0	0	0.00		39	0							
	1894		2	4	0	66	42	16.50										
Handford, A.	1894		2	4	0	46	36	11.50										
	1894	1915	1	2	2	5	5*	–		83	4		20.75	3/61				
Henson, R.	1886	1891	26	38	9	275	24*	9.48		1722	60		28.70	7/39	5		16	
	1886	1891	1	2	0	19	17	9.50		5	2		2.50	2/5				
Holden, C.	1886	1894	5	9	0	93	45	10.33		52	1		52.00	1/29			5	
	1885	1894	8	14	1	136	45	10.46		63	1		63.00	1/29			6	
Hornby, E.C.	1892	1893	4	7	0	131	46	18.71		79	3		26.33	2/23			3	
	1892	1893	13	20	1	360	82	18.94		177	6		29.50	2/23			9	
			2	4	0	77	67	19.25									2	2
Hubback, T.R.			6	10	1	140	67	15.55									3	2

	First	Last	M	I	NO	Runs	HS	Avg	100	Runs	Wkts	OW	Avg	Best	5i	10m	ct	st
Jones, C.L.	1882	1890	6	12	0	113	36	9.41										
	1876	1890	11	22	1	165	36	7.85		6	1		6.00	1/6				
Jones, F.J.	1889		1	2	0	13	12	6.50		71	4		17.75	4/71				
Kemble, A.T.	1887	1894	6	12	1	107	23	9.72									5	3
	1885	1896	95	144	23	1347	50	11.13									122	54
Leach, H.	1884	1891	2	4	1	68	46	22.66		4	0						1	
	1881	1891	3	5	1	101	46	25.25		4	0						2	
MacLaren, A.C.	1892	1894	4	8	0	295	84	36.87									3	
	1890	1921	424	703	52	22236	424	34.15	47	267	1		267.00	1/44			453	
Morgan, W.A.	1889		1	2	0	2	2	1.00										
Moss, R.H.	1893		1	2	0	13	13	6.50		23	0							
	1887	1925	16	28	10	123	18*	6.83		886	25		35.44	4/9			11	
Oakley, W.	1892	1894	4	7	2	13	9	2.60		335	18		18.61	5/29	3	1	1	
	1892	1894	24	38	10	144	24	5.14		973	55		17.69	6/50	5	1	21	
Patterson, W.S.	1882		1	2	0	1	1	0.50		16	0							
	1874	1882	41	66	5	1114	105*	18.26	1	2330	158	5	14.74	7/30	17	5	20	
Pilling, R.	1882		1	2	0	5	3	2.50									2	
	1877	1889	250	372	111	2572	78	9.85									459	208
Porter, E.H.	1882		1	2	0	9	6	4.50										
	1874	1883	20	34	1	374	61	11.33		48	3		16.00	3/28			13	
Price, A.	1884		1	2	0	38	37	19.00									1	
	1884	1887	7	12	0	110	37	9.16									7	
Price, W.	1889		2	4	2	28	26*	14.00		113	10		11.30	6/51	1		1	
Ratcliffe, E.	1886	1889	3	5	0	58	28	11.60		35	1		35.00	1/10			2	
	1884	1889	4	7	0	67	28	9.57		43	1		43.00	1/10			2	
Ravenscroft, James	1888	1894	2	4	0	0	0	0.00									2	
Richardson, H.	1887	1889	3	6	1	77	55	15.40		217	18		12.05	7/46	2		1	
	1887	1894	65	91	14	664	55	8.62		2545	185		13.75	7/24	10	1	44	
Roper, E.	1891	1893	2	4	0	29	19	7.25		6	1		6.00	1/6			1	
	1876	1893	36	59	3	715	68	12.76		6	1		6.00	1/6			9	
Royle, V.P.F.A.	1882		1	2	0	14	12	7.00									1	
	1873	1891	102	165	15	2322	81	15.48		376	15		25.06	4/51			69	
Shore, C.	1886	1887	2	3	2	86	42*	86.00		203	10		20.30	4/45			1	
	1881	1887	13	21	9	159	42*	13.25		938	41		22.87	5/36	2		9	
Shoubridge, T.E.	1890		1	2	2	4	4*	-		45	1		45.00	1/35				
	1890		3	6	2	14	10	3.50		77	1		77.00	1/35				
Smith, Albert	1894		2	4	0	38	21	9.50		170	7		24.28	4/57			1	
Smith, Edwin	1886	1894	9	17	3	118	32	8.42		487	25		19.48	7/59	1	1	5	
Steel, A.G.	1882	1894	14	26	0	822	100	31.61	1	699	36		19.41	4/46			18	
	1877	1895	162	261	23	7000	171	29.41	8	11665	789		14.78	9/63	64	20	137	
Steel, D.Q.	1882	1886	3	5	0	13	9	2.60									1	1
	1876	1887	57	89	3	1674	158	19.46	1	173	7		24.71	5/65	1		28	4
Steel, E.E.	1887	1893	2	4	0	56	25	14.00		10	0						1	
	1884	1904	47	69	4	1133	111	17.43	1	2877	129	2	22.30	6/69	11	2	42	
Steel, H.B.	1884	1894	12	23	0	244	48	10.60		81	1		81.00	1/15			11	
	1883	1896	36	63	3	1042	100	17.36	1	83	1		83.00	1/15			20	

	First	Last	M	I	NO	Runs	HS	Avg	100	Runs	Wkts	OW	Avg	Best	5i	10m	ct	st
Stubbs, T.A.	1893	1894	4	8	1	168	43	24.00									2	
Sugg, F.H.	1893	1899	1	2	0	18	14	9.00									2	
	1883		305	515	30	11859	220	24.45	16	273	10		27.30	2/12			167	1
Thompson, J.C.P.	1892		1	1		14	14	14.00									1	
Thompson, W.H.	1892	1884	1	1	0	10	10	10.00		24	1		24.00	1/24				
Watson, A.	1882	1893	2	4	0	38	19	12.66		82	1		82.00	1/18			1	
	1871		303	453	96	4492	74	12.58		18423	1384		13.31	9/118	106	27	277	
White, J.	1886	1890	2	3	0	11	6	3.66									3	2
	1886	1890	3	4	2	73	62	18.25		166	5		33.20	2/40			4	2
Whitehead, S.J.	1891	1892	2	3	2	25	17*	25.00									1	
	1891		58	78	29	519	46	10.59		4380	183		23.93	8/47	11	4	34	
Wood, R.	1884	1900	1	2		8	7*	8.00										
	1880		12	20	5	235	52	15.66		36	4		9.00	3/19			5	
Woodward, E.	1888	1887	2	4	0	19	13	4.75		134	8		16.75	3/19			1	
Young, W.	1891	1890	1	2	0	21	21*	21.00		50	2		25.00	2/38			1	

Where two lines of figures are shown the first line is for first-class matches for Liverpool & District and the second line is all first-class matches.

GENTLEMEN OF LIVERPOOL (& DISTRICT) NON FIRST-CLASS CAREER RECORDS

	First	Last	M	I	NO	Runs	HS	Avg	100	Runs	Wkts	OW	Avg	Best	5i	10m	ct	st
Ainslie, Rev. R.M.	1889		1	2	0	9	6	4.50										
Ashworth, W.	1888		1	1	0	0	0	0.00										
Barnes, W.P.	1911		1	2	0	40	40	20.00		34	0						2	
Baucher, F.W.	1910	1911	2	3	2	11	7*	11.00		60	9		6.66	5/23	1		1	1
	1903		3	2	0	12	8	6.00		47	1		47.00	1/47				
Bird, G.	1884	1889	3	6	0	133	35	22.16		12	1		12.00	1/12			6	5
	1872	1880	21	36	3	477	75	14.45		0	0							
Blease, H.	1910		1	1	0	7	5	3.50										
Bowring, F.H.	1910		1	2	0	8	8	8.00										
Bowring, W.	1911		1	1	0	30	30	15.00									2	
Brancker, C.H.	1888		1	1	0	0	0	0.00										
Chadwick, Rev.R.M.	1910		2	2	0	40	22	20.00										
Cunningham, J.C.	1910	1911	1	4	1	44	20*	14.66		4	0							
Cunningham, R.	1911		1	2	0	58	37	29.00		32	0							
Dunlop, R.G.	1884		1	2	0	6	3	3.00									1	
Eccles, A.P.	1888		1	1	1	3	3*	-		61	9		6.77	5/25	1		2	

Name	First	Last	M	I	NO	Runs	HS	Avg	100	Runs	Wkts	OW	Avg	Best	5i	10m	ct	st
Evans, T.	1887		1	1	0	0	0	0.00		94	11		8.54	6/58	2	1	2	2
Field, S.	1889		1	2	0	2	2	1.00		42	1		42.00	1/42				
Fraser, W.	1911		1	2	0	11	7	5.50		17	0							
Hannay, C.S.	1910		1	2	0	32	28	16.00		61	8		7.62	7/31	1			
	1901			2	0	24	20	12.00										
Holden, C.	1887		1	2	0	65	64	32.50		25	1		25.00	1/25			1	
Hornby, E.C.	1884	1889	3	6	1	97	64	19.40		198	10		19.80	5/86	1		5	
Hornby, G.F.	1884		1	2	0	0	0	0.00		34	3		11.33	2/19			4	
	1882			2	1	1	1	0.50										
Hornby, J.	1889		1	2	1	5	5*	5.00		64	1		64.00	1/64			1	
Johnson, T.H.	1911		1	2	0	4	3	2.00		18	0						1	
Jones, C.L.	1887		1	2	1	52	29*	52.00		33	2		16.50	2/33				
Jones, F.	1887		1	1	1	2	2*	-										
Jones, F.A.	1910		1	2	0	23	20	11.50		18	1		18.00	1/18			4	
Kemble, A.T.	1887	1889	3	5	0	71	36	35.20									1	
Kirby, E.F.J.	1911		1	2	0	15	8	7.50		34	1		34.00	1/34				2
Leach, H.	1889		1	2	0	32	26	16.00		66	0						1	
Lott, F.	1910		1	2	0	1	1	1.00		50	4		12.50	3/29			1	
Manson, E.	1884		1	2	0	19	19	9.50		35	3		11.66	2/6				
Morrice, K.D.R.	1910		3	4	1	71	50	35.50		61	2		30.50	2/45				
Nicholson, G.	1887	1889	2	3	0	35	30*	11.66		60	0						5	
O'Dwyer, J.B.	1888	1889	2	4	0	52	26	17.33		41	0						1	
O'Dwyer, W.M.P.	1888	1889	1	4	0	27	10	6.75									1	
Parr, H.B.	1884		1	2	0	51	46	25.50										
	1872		11	16	0	180	61	11.25									4	
Potter, W.H.	1884	1876	1	2	0	41	32	41.00									1	2
	1870		1	2	0	23	12	11.50										
Ratcliffe, Harold	1887		1	1	0	32	32	32.00									1	
Ravenscroft, James	1887		1	2	0	4	4	2.00										
Rimmer, F.A.	1910	1911	2	3	1	10	6*	5.00		173	11		15.72	5/89	1		2	
Roper, E.	1884	1888	3	6	0	67	41	11.16		23	1		23.00	1/9				
Roughton, L.K	1888		1	2	1	13	9	13.00									4	
Smith, J.W.	1911		1	2	0	5	3	2.50										
Steel, E.E.	1884		1	2	1	7	7	7.00		77	3		25.66	3/77				
Steel, H.B.	1884	1889	4	8	0	174	77	21.75		74	6		12.33	4/50			3	
Swift, Rev. J.M.	1911		1	2	0	21	16	10.50		85	1		85.00	1/24				
Williams, G.L.	1910		1	2	0	35	35	35.00		28	0							
Wood, R.	1884		1	2	0	24	13	12.00		84	7		12.00	4/35			1	

Where two lines of figures are shown the first line is for non first-class matches for Gentlemen of Liverpool (& District) and the second line is all first-class matches if not given in the previous table.

LIVERPOOL & DISTRICT NON FIRST-CLASS CAREER RECORDS

Name	First	Last	M	I	NO	Runs	HS	Avg	100	Runs	Wkts	OW	Avg	Best	5i	10m	ct	st
Adams, L.P.B.	1947		1	2	0	36	29	18.00										
Ainscough, H.	1894		1	2	0	11	9	5.50										
Ainscough, John	1895		2	3	0	41	33	13.66									3	
Ainscough, T.	1894	1904	18	34	0	958	195	28.17	1								13	
Ainsworth, J.L.	1896		1	2	0	11	10	5.50		18	1		18.00	1/18				
Allen, W.G.	1899	1904	11	16	5	44	11	4.00		791	50		15.82	7/61	5	2	7	
Ashcroft, E.	1947		1	2	0	12	11	6.00										
Bardswell, G.R.	1894	1902	3	5	1	83	51*	20.75		94	3		31.33	3/85			3	
Barnes, J.R.	1894	1902	59	92	13	1585	97	20.06		1618	63		25.68	6/36	4		104	
	1902	1932	2	3	0	90	48	30.00		53	0						1	
Barnes, W.P.	1919	1931	94	145	23	3643	133	29.86	4								40	
Barrell, B.	1896	1907	17	33	0	898	86	27.21		521	19		27.42	5/46	1		13	
	1911	1923	1	1	0	19	19	19.00		89	1		89.00	1/19			1	
Bates, W.E.	1923	1932	3	3	1	45	25	22.50		135	9		15.00	3/10				
	1932		1	1	0	111	111	111.00	1									
Baucher, F.W.	1907	1931	406	684	30	15964	200*	24.40	13	8671	230		37.70	8/93	4	1	250	6
Blackburn, W.E.	1906	1920	3	6	1	43	31	7.16		91	10		9.10	6/50	1		5	
	1920		1	1	0	7	7*	7.00									1	
Blease, H.	1919	1920	10	13	6	26	6*	3.71		1113	45		24.73	5/17	4	1	9	
Boswell, A.H.	1906	1907	2	4	0	27	14	6.75		163	4		40.75	2/44			1	
Boumphrey, D.	1904	1905	1	3	1	25	12*	12.50									2	
	1928		1	2	0	17		8.50										
Bowring, F.H.	1901	1903	2	2	0	10	6	5.00		276	12		23.00	4/70			2	
Bretherton, J.	1895	1898	3	5	1	38	23	9.50		296	15		19.73	8/42	2		1	
Brock, A.W.	1904		1	4	2	19	5*	6.33		1	1		1.00					
Brocklebank, E.	1905		1	2	0	17	17	8.50		82	2		41.00	2/82				
Brocklebank, Sir J.M.	1947		1	2	0	32	22	16.00										
	1936	1949	21	26	14	112	23	9.33		1998	68		29.38	6/92	4	2	7	
Brown, H.S.	1932		1	1	0	67	67	67.00										
Brown, J.H.	1904	1907	3	6	1	56	30*	11.20		257	12		21.41	4/45			2	
	1898	1905	15	28	3	305	53*	12.20		325	7		46.42	2/6			16	
Burrough, Rev. J.	1900	1902	4	7	0	181	62	25.85		312	14		22.28	4/42			5	
	1893	1914	24	39	5	780	127	22.94									15	
Cole, T.G.O.	1901	1903	4	8	0	387	116	48.37	1	1929	65		29.67	6/29	4	2	3	
	1898	1922	20	35	3	499	68	15.59		114	6		19.00	4/74			9	
Court, L.	1906		1	2	2	2	1*	–		17	0							
Crosfield, S.M.	1895		1	2	0	8	8	4.00		33	0							
Cunningham, R.	1920		1	2	0	29	17	14.50		32	0							
Duckham, W.	1932		1	1	0	9	9	9.00		64	9		7.11	5/41	1		1	
Garnett, H.G.	1899	1904	10	19	0	635	97	33.42		80	1		80.00	1/4			13	
	1899	1914	152	245	22	5798	139	26.00	5	224	8		28.00	2/18			185	18

Cricket register (batting and bowling averages).

Name	First	Last	M	I	NO	Runs	HS	Avg	100	Runs	Wkts	OW	Avg	Best 1/8	5i	10m	ct	st
Goodwin, F.H.	1899		1	2	1	13	13*	13.00		8	1	1	8.00				2	
	1894		3	6	1	14	10	2.80		47	0	0						
Graham, A.J.	1906		1	2	0	119	86	59.50									1	
Grayson, J.H.F.	1895		1	2	1	17	16	17.00										
Greenhalgh, E.W.	1947		1	2	0	31	29	15.50										
	1935	1938	14	18	5	366	53*	28.15		282	3		94.00	2/75			2	
Gregory, J.C.	1900	1904	3	5	4	40	15*	40.00		229	5		45.80	5/111	1		1	
Grewcock, G.	1902		3	1	0	8	8	8.00		28	1		28.00	1/28				
	1899		2	6	0	4	1	0.66		308	8		38.50	4/93				4
Hampshire, G.N.	1904	1905	5	3	0	5	5	1.66									1	
Hancock, H.B.	1903	1907	1	10	0	170	50	17.00		85	3		28.33	2/10			3	
Handford, A.	1894		5	2	0	14	13	7.00									2	
Hannay, C.S.	1903		1	10	2	233	42	29.12		53	2		26.50	1/7				
Henson, R.	1898	1907	1	2	0	23	13	11.50		50	1		50.00	1/34			3	
Hickmott, W.E.	1932		1	1	1	12	12*	-		111	2		55.50	1/29				
Hilton, W.H.	1914	1924	37	40	11	301	31*	10.37		2360	92		25.65	5/20	2		25	
Hodgson, H.W.	1894	1896	4	8	2	57	22*	9.50		23	1		-				3	
Holden, C.	1920	1932	2	3	0	82	56	27.33		86	1		86.00	1/17			1	
	1924	1927	2	4	0	79	45	19.75										
Home, H.	1895	1901	8	16	1	484	172	32.26	1	33	1		33.00	1/12			9	
	1894		1	2	1	4	4*	4.00										
Hornby, E.C.	1901		1	2	0	105	70	52.50		26	1		26.00	1/26				
Howard, Dr. W.	1932		1	1	0	20	20	20.00										
	1895		3	2	0	13	13	6.50		158	4		39.50	2/72			2	
Hubback, T.R.	1896		1	6	1	136	65*	27.20										
Hutton, C.F.	1920	1898	3	2	0	33	28	16.50		4	0	0					1	
Johnson, E.F.H.	1900		1	6	0	101	31	16.83									2	
Johnston, J.D.	1894	1901	3	30	4	312	59	12.00									23	
Kemble, A.T.	1897	1903	16	2	0	65	38	32.50		42	3		14.00	3/26			2	
King, J.H.	1895	1925	552	988	69	25122	227*	27.33	34	30312	1204		25.17	8/17	69	11	340	13
Kirby, E.F.J.	1900	1902	2	4	2	72	29	36.00		58	1		58.00	1/15			1	
Kitchener, F.G.	1901	1905	7	13	2	76	21	6.90		889	36		24.69	6/86	2		2	
	1896	1903	13	19	3	80	16	5.00		630	28		22.50	6/59	2		6	
Lashmar, J.W.T.	1898		1	2	0	16	9	8.00		19	1		19.00	1/19				
Leach, H.	1898	1903	4	2	0	44	41	22.00		44	0							
Leather, A.B.	1901		36	8	0	137	67	17.12		71	0						3	
Legard, A.R.	1947	1952	1	1	1	2	2*	-										
	1932			52	10	234	38	5.57										
Lister, W.H.L.	1933	1939		2	0	57	54	28.50									17	
	1894		162	218	17	3709	104*	18.45	2	2793	93		30.03	7/36	3		73	
Lorrimer, D.A.	1906		1	2	0	76	48	38.00		87	1		87.00	1/10			1	
McCormick, Rev. J.G.	1920		1	2	0	75	61	37.50										
McEntyre, D.P.	1947			2	0	34	24	17.00										
McEntyre, G.A.	1920		1	2	0	22	17	11.00		30	0							
McLeod, K.G.	1908	1914	94	2	0	39	32	19.50									2	
				161	16	3458	131	23.84	6	2748	103		26.67	6/29	2	1	107	2

30

	First	Last	M	I	NO	Runs	HS	Avg	100	Runs	Wkts	OW	Avg	Best	5i	10m	ct	st
Makepeace, J.W.H.	1907		1	2	0	17	16	8.50									1	
	1906	1930	499	778	66	25799	203	36.23	43	1971	42		46.92	4/33			194	
Mason, P.	1902	1907	4	8	2	44	18	7.33		222	8		27.75	6/24	1		6	
	1896	1901	43	64	10	879	80	16.27		402	10		40.20	2/20			7	
Morrice, K.D.R.	1905	1906	2	4	1	118	91*	39.33		170	3		56.66	1/16			3	
Needham, E.	1898		1	2	0	27	20	13.50		79	2		39.50	2/79				
Nicholas, F.W.H.	1932		1	1	0	17	17	17.00									1	
	1912	1929	76	122	5	2634	140	22.51	1								51	16
Nutter, A.E.	1932		1	1	0	28	28	28.00		65	2		32.50	1/24				
	1935	1953	224	294	47	4828	109*	19.54	1	15739	600		26.23	7/52	29	2	161	
Oakley, W.	1895	1897	3	5	1	24	21	6.00		376	15		25.06	5/132	1		5	
O'Hara, Dr. W.E.	1905		1	1	0	38	38	38.00		65	1		65.00	1/43			2	
Peel, L.G.	1901		1	2	0	29	18	14.50									1	
Pilkington, C.C.	1899		1	2	0	41	34	20.50									1	
	1895	1919	13	20	1	468	86	24.63		370	9		41.11	3/70			6	
Pilkington, H.C.	1900		1	2	1	80	68*	80.00										
	1899	1904	20	30	2	688	93	24.57		16	0						7	
Price, W.	1896		1	2	0	2	2	1.00		69	2		34.50	2/20				
Rapkin, G.J.	1920		1	2	0	20	11	10.00										
Rimmer, F.A.	1902	1906	6	12	3	48	11*	5.33		699	22		31.77	4/78			2	
Ringrose, W.	1895	1900	6	10	4	79	29	13.16		525	34		15.44	8/47	3	1	1	
	1901	1912	61	74	11	377	23	5.98		3568	175		20.38	9/76	11	2	27	
Sharp, J.	1895		1	2	1	32	32*	32.00		14	0							
	1899	1925	534	805	75	22715	211	31.11	38	12088	441		27.41	9/77	18	3	236	
Shepherd, S.G.	1947		1	1	1	11	11*	-		73	5		14.60	5/73	1		1	
	1936		1	2	0	9	9	4.50		4	0							
Shutt, T.	1901		1	1	0	18	18	18.00		24	0		-					
Smith, Albert	1894	1895	3	5	0	25	14	5.00		139	5		27.80	4/56			4	
Spooner, A.F.	1904	1906	3	6	0	136	50	22.66		45	0							
	1906	1909	18	33	1	500	83	15.62									8	
Spooner, R.H.	1903		1	2	0	61	34	30.50										
	1899	1923	237	393	16	13681	247	36.28	31	582	6		97.00	1/5			142	
Steel, E.E.	1901	1907	6	12	0	337	77	28.08		569	35		16.25	7/95	3	1	13	
Steel, H.B.	1894	1904	6	12	1	353	91*	32.09		26	0						1	
Stoddart, W.B.	1896	1920	7	14	4	221	56*	22.10		457	25		18.28	6/78	3	1	7	
	1898	1899	19	32	5	410	43*	15.18		1122	48		23.37	6/121	3		7	
Stott, A.	1899	1904	8	15	0	146	24	9.73		483	10		48.30	3/48			6	
Stubbs, T.A.	1894	1895	3	6	1	144	50	28.80									2	
Sugg, F.H.	1897		1	2	0	57	55	28.50									1	
Sugg, W.	1896	1897	2	4	0	40	21	10.00		43	2		21.50	1/16			2	
	1881	1902	129	218	16	3469	107	17.17	2	1560	50		31.20	4/61			64	
Taylor, R.H.M.	1903	1907	2	4	0	35	17	8.75										
Thompson, F.G.	1901	1905	2	3	0	7	6	2.33		71	6		11.83	6/55	1		1	
Tyler, R.	1947		1	2	1	10	9	10.00		46	1		46.00	1/46				
Warlow, C.A.	1932		1	1	0	14	14	14.00										

	First	Last	M	I	NO	Runs	HS	Avg	100	Runs	Wkts	OW	Avg	Best	5i	10m	ct	st
Warlow, C.M.	1904		1	2	0	57	54	28.50		176	5		35.20	4/114			1	
Warren, A.(R.)	1901		1	2	0	28	20	14.00										
	1897	1920	255	445	44	5507	123	13.73	1	23061	939		24.55	8/69	72	15	195	
Weaver, F.W.H.	1904		1	2	0	17	17	8.50									1	
Wilson, C.E.	1905		1	2	1	83	78*	83.00		8	1		8.00	1/8			1	
Wolstenholme, A.M.	1947		1	2	0	38	24	19.00									2	

Where two lines of figures are shown the first line is for non first-class matches for Liverpool & District and the second line is all first-class matches if not given in either of the previous tables.